▲▲

A FIELD GUIDE
TO THE
U.S. ECONOMY

The Center for Popular Economics

COORDINATED AND WRITTEN BY NANCY FOLBRE

Pantheon Books   New York

Grateful acknowledgment is made to the following for
permission to reprint previously published material:
LOS ANGELES TIMES SYNDICATE: Wasserman cartoons:
"Let me explain the relationship...," "Unemployment rate,"
"On Wall Street Today...," and "If You Poor Nations Want
More..." Copyright © 1981, 1983, 1984, 1986 by
the *Boston Globe.* "There seem to be more and more people
sleeping in the streets...," and "This is our mission—We
will run an operation against Nicaragua that violates U.S. law..."
Copyright © 1987 by the *Boston Globe.* Reprinted by permission
of the *Los Angeles Times* Syndicate
ST. MARTIN'S PRESS, INC.: Cartoons from *My Weight Is Always
Perfect for My Height—Which Varies,* and *Mercy, It's the
Revolution and I'm in My Bathrobe,* by Nicole Hollander.
Copyright © 1982 by Nicole Hollander. Reprinted by
permission of St. Martin's Press, Inc., New York.

Library of Congress Cataloging-in-Publication Data
Center for Popular Economics
A field guide to the U.S. economy.

Bibliography: p.
1. United States—Economic conditions.   2. Economic
indicators—United States.   I. Center for
Popular Economics (U.S.)
HC103.F44   1987   330.973   86-42974
ISBN 0-349-75047-0 (pbk.)

Manufactured in the United States of America
468975

CONTENTS

▲ ▲

CHAPTER TEN: THE GLOBAL ECONOMY

TOOLKIT

SOURCES

GLOSSARY

ACKNOWLEDGMENTS

▲▲

*M*any different minds and hands have shaped every page in this book. My pleasure, as coordinator and writer, is to give credit and say thanks. First, I celebrate the collective commitment of the staff members of the Center for Popular Economics, whose practical teaching experience inspired this book, and whose dedicated research made it possible. We are:

Randy Albelda, Massachusetts Senate Committee on Taxation
Masato Aoki, University of Massachusetts
Samuel Bowles, University of Massachusetts
Kim Christensen, State University of New York at Purchase
Gerald Epstein, New School for Social Research
Terianne Falcone, Westfield State College
Diane Flaherty, University of Massachusetts
Nancy Folbre, University of Massachusetts
Jetta Fraser, University of Massachusetts
Julie Graham, University of Massachusetts
Curtis Haynes, University of Massachusetts
Glen Hutloff, University of Massachusetts
Marc Kitchel, University of Massachusetts
David Kotz, University of Massachusetts
June Lapidus, University of Massachusetts

Elaine McCrate, University of Vermont
Terry McDonough, Conitius College
Edwin Meléndez, Massachusetts Institute of Technology
Manuel Pastor, Occidental College
Karen Pfeifer, Smith College
Jim Rebitzer, University of Texas
Tom Riddell, Smith College
Julie Schor, Harvard University
James Stormes, St. Joseph's University
Brenda Wyss, University of Massachusetts
Lyuba Zarsky, University of Massachusetts

On behalf of the Center for Popular Economics, I gratefully acknowledge the contributions and suggestions of Constance Blake, Peter Bohmer, James Boyce, Mark Breibart, Barbara Briggs, Elaine Burns, Duane Campbell, James Crotty, Vine Deloria, Jr., Peter Dorman, Bob Dworak, Myrick Freeman III, Eric Fure, Barbara Goldaftas, David Gordon, Betsy Hartman, Beth Lait, Jonathan Lash, David Levine, Jeanine Maland, Regina Markey, Judy Robinson, Gene Severens, William G. Shepherd, Steven Shulman, Helen Smith, Elaine Sorensen, Steve Stamos, Phillip Stern, Tom Weisskopf, and Josh Winder. Thanks to the Presbyterian Church (U.S.A.) and to the United Methodist

▲ ▲

Church (national division), whose financial assistance enabled us to complete this book.

The following groups and individuals have helped fund CPE's programs since 1978: Beacon Fund/National Community Funds; Bread and Roses Community Fund; CarEth Foundation; Circle Fund; Discount Foundation; the Domestic and Foreign Missionary Society of the Protestant Episcopal Church in the USA; Economics and Democratic Values Project; Evergreen Fund; the Fairtree Foundation; W.H. & Carol Bernstein Ferry; Field Foundation; Fund for Tomorrow; Funding Exchange/National Community Funds; General Board of Global Ministries (the United Methodist Church); General Funding Committee/National Community Funds; Haymarket Peoples' Fund; Holy Cross Fathers (Eastern Province); Max and Anna Levinson Foundation; the Limantour Foundation; Peace Development Fund; the Philadelphia Foundation; Presbyterian Church (U.S.A.); Public Concern Foundation; PBP Foundation; RESIST; Samuel Rubin Foundation; Sisters of the Humility of Mary; Sisters of Loretto; Shalan Foundation; the Sunflower Foundation; a Territory Resource; Twenty-First Century Foundation; United Church Board for Homeland Ministries (United Church of Christ); Windom Fund; Women's Opportunity Giving Fund of the Presbyterian Church in the U.S.A.; and the Youth Project.

A special thanks to our administrators, present and past: Natasha Harmon, Valerie LePere, Melissa Robbins, and Katie Williamson, for their perseverance and dedication, and to Susan Ells, our irrepressible fundraiser.

Thanks to Howard Saunders, who not only drew most of the illustrations but advised on overall design from the very beginning. His imagination was an inspiration to everyone who worked on the book. Thanks also to Nicole Hollander and Dan Wasserman for their wonderful cartoons.

I am personally indebted to Michael Barnes, who worked closely with me during the early and most difficult stages of this project and helped shepherd it almost to completion. Four excellent research assistants contributed considerable time and energy: Kate Boland, Andrea DeVries, Nancy Gutman, and Barnet Wagman. Special thanks to Collective Copies of Amherst, Massachusetts, for their cooperative spirit, and to Bill Thompson and other government-documents librarians at the University of Massachusetts for their friendly and expert assistance.

Finally, here's to Maurilio Ortiz, who got me started on this, I think, years ago, and to my softball team, the Bats, who taught me much of what I know about good teamwork.

Nancy Folbre

INTRODUCTION: WHAT'S THE BOTTOM LINE?

*I*f there were just one bottom line, the U.S. economy would be easier to understand. Like one big checking account, we could just look at our monthly statement to see how we were doing. We could see who made the deposits and who made the withdrawals and figure out who got what, and why.

It's not so simple, because an economy is more than a set of accounts. It's a system of production. People put in their labor, their talents, and a little bit of their soul, and they take out their livelihood. Some people get rich, some people get poor; sometimes the overall economy grows, sometimes it falters. Not even the best economists in the world understand exactly how it works.

But most people want to know more about it, if only because they're worried about the bottom lines in their own checkbooks. The income of the typical U.S. family has hardly increased over the past five years, despite the growing number of women working outside the home. Many families have experienced unemployment. Some families haven't been able to pay their bills.

People are also worried about the larger economic trends affecting their communities, their country, and their world: increased unemployment and major plant closings, continued racial and sexual inequality, greater poverty and homelessness, major environmental accidents and problems, large debts hanging over U.S. farmers and developing countries across the globe. Rather than addressing these problems, the Reagan administration has done its best to ignore them.

Many people would like to develop their concerns about the economy into constructive criticisms and practical proposals for change. They often find it difficult to do so, partly because economics is complicated and partly because economists aren't very good explaining it. There's another important difficulty: those who know a great deal about the U.S. economy are often exceedingly fond of it. Economic experts are far more likely to extol the virtues of the U.S. economy than to encourage criticisms of it.

Prevailing orthodoxy holds that the economy does not need critics or watchdogs of any sort and, indeed, works much better without them. Typical economics courses confine their attention to the theory of competitive markets and treat the economy as a self-regulating system with a built-in balance of power. Even economists who address issues of public policy often teach students that social equity gets in the way of efficiency. In short, social justice is just too expensive.

Some economists disagree. They believe that economic power in the U.S. is unevenly distributed and easily abused, and that current economic policies are inefficient as well as unfair. They also believe that good citizens should be good critics, that controversy and debate over economic issues are central to the meaning of political democracy. But whatever their political views, economists tend to spend most of their time arguing with other economists, rather than encouraging ordinary people to participate in the economic debate.

With this book, the Center for Popular Economics intended something different. We set out to compile important information for people who want to join that debate because they are concerned about where the U.S. economy is heading. The facts and figures we highlight and illustrate here reflect our personal values and our political concerns. But we do not develop a single interpretation of U.S. economic trends or advocate any particular economic policies. Our aim is not to persuade but to inform and provoke, to enlighten and enliven economic debate.

We titled this book *A Field Guide to the U.S. Economy* because we wanted to convey its dual purpose: to serve as an accessible, concise reference for answering specific questions and to provide an informative overview of the U.S. economy as a whole. Each page stands alone as a description of a particular economic fact or trend, but it also fits into a chapter that systematically covers a particular topic. You might want to read the book from cover to cover. Or you might want to scan the page titles in the table of contents for one that interests you, and then follow your nose. At the bottom of each page a "see also" note points you to related charts in other chapters.

Each of the first five chapters explains the economic position and history of an important group of people: owners, workers, women, people of color, and farmers. Each of the next five chapters covers a particular area of concern: government spending, welfare, education and health, energy and environment, macroeconomics, and the global economy. The later chapters, the last two in particular, are more difficult than the other ones.

Each chapter opens with a brief overview tying its charts together around a main theme. The pages tend to progress from the general to the specific, providing a variety of types of information—descriptions of widely discussed trends, explanations of basic economic concepts, and occasionally more speculative analyses of possibilities for change. While most of the charts trace one economic variable over time, some examine the relationship between important variables. In order to provide an overiew of the post–

World War II period, we tracked historical data back to 1950 whenever feasible.

The main text of the book is followed by a toolkit. Its ten sections will help readers interpret and use economic statistics. They include reminders about how to read graphs and explanations of things like price indices and the poverty line. Certain charts are keyed at the bottom of the page to the toolkit sections.

The first toolkit section provides a general guide to sources of economic data. The detailed bibliographic sources that follow the toolkit constitute a specific guide that will facilitate updating of the charts. Finally, the glossary provides simple definitions of many technical terms.

For the past eight years, the Center for Popular Economics has organized and taught classes and workshops on economic issues for community organizers and activists. Our students constantly demanded more information, more explanation, more documentation.

Every year we added to a pile of classroom handouts; every year we found it harder to keep our pile organized and up-to-date.

In the summer of 1984, we transferred our handouts to computer files and began to experiment with computer generated graphs. Our students loved the results. "Make it a book," they exclaimed, "but make it more fun." Economists always have a hard time doing that, but our students' enthusiasm fanned our ambition to produce a readable critical guide to the U.S. economy.

Every member of the Center for Popular Economics contributed to this book. Many past participants in our summer programs provided detailed suggestions. Many colleagues who share our interest in promoting economic literacy also lent us a hand. All of us shared a common purpose, a commitment to a kind of economics that is popular, in the best sense of the word. It's for ordinary people.

That's our bottom line.

$\mathcal{W}$ho owns what in the United States? This chapter looks at the distribution of family wealth and the structure of corporate power. It also takes a short glance at some ways the ownership of wealth might be changed.

Them that has, gets. Individuals compete against each other in the capitalist marketplace, but their success is partly determined by what they bring with them to the market. Some people bring nothing but their skills. Others bring considerable wealth, and when they leave the marketplace, they usually take home even more. Chart 1.1 shows that families with low and middle incomes have far lower levels of accumulated wealth than those ranked by income in the top 10%. But there are even bigger differences in wealth within that upper-income group. As Chart 1.2 points out, the very wealthiest individuals in the U.S. are more than a thousand times richer than the average high-income person.

Most families with low and middle incomes use their earnings to buy things like a house or a car. But the very wealthy enjoy substantial income from the ownership of income-producing assets like stocks, bonds, and investment properties. As Chart 1.3 shows, this group is a small minority. Only 2% of adults received more than $10,000 in property income in 1983. Chart 1.4 helps explain why. Stocks and bonds are concentrated in relatively few hands.

Wealth can buy more than a high standard of living. Sometimes political influence and economic power come up for sale. Chart 1.5 details the increasingly important role that large contributions play in determining electoral outcomes, while Chart 1.6 answers a hypothetical question: How much actual control of the economy could wealth buy?

Corporations exercise far more economic power than individuals or families. When they compete fiercely with one another, their individual influence is limited. But as the next six charts show, competition isn't always the rule. Chart 1.7 pictures four major industries that are dominated by two or three firms, and Chart 1.8 documents an increase in the relative size of the largest one hundred corporations over time.

Charts 1.9 and 1.10 show that big corporations often grow by taking over smaller ones. In the recent wave of mergers and acquisitions, corporations spent enormous sums of money that could have been devoted to increasing their own productive capacity. U.S. antitrust law has always held that "mere size is no offense."

Still, the size of some economic institutions is awesome. The top ten commercial banks loom over the smaller regional banks (Chart 1.11), and many multinational corporations have total sales that far exceed the value of goods and services produced in many developing countries (Chart 1.12).

But perhaps these institutions are less monolithic than they seem. The employee stock-ownership plans described in Chart 1.13 haven't given workers much control over corporate wealth but might in the future. And while few workers enjoy any control over their pension funds, the figures in Chart 1.14 suggest how powerful that kind of control could be.

1.1 ☐ WEALTH AND INCOME IN THE U.S.

*W*ealth and income often go together in the U.S. economy, but they are not the same thing. Wealth is an accumulation of money and assets that can be sold for money. Income is a flow of money received over a certain period of time, such as profits or earnings. Net worth is the value of savings, investments, and property, minus debts.

Among the top 10% of families ranked by income, the typical family in 1983 had a net worth of about $130,851.

Families with low and middle income have a far lower net worth, and most of their wealth takes the form of home ownership rather than savings or investments that can generate income.

The distribution of wealth in the U.S. has remained almost constant since 1950, but a recent congressional study suggests that it became more unequal in the mid-1980s.

SEE ALSO 7.2

Median Wealth of Families by Income Level, 1983

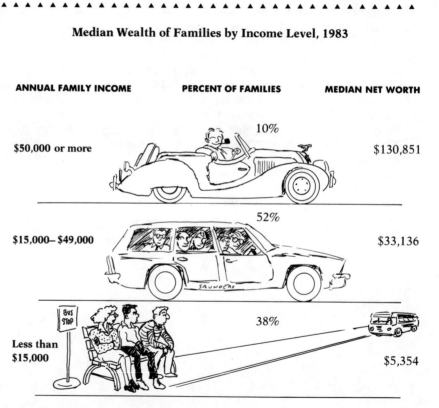

ANNUAL FAMILY INCOME	PERCENT OF FAMILIES	MEDIAN NET WORTH
$50,000 or more	10%	$130,851
$15,000–$49,000	52%	$33,136
Less than $15,000	38%	$5,354

Sam Moore Walton

Henry Ross Perot

David Packard

Margaret Hunt Hill

Caroline Rose Hunt Schoellkopf

The twenty richest people in the U.S. in 1985 were all worth more than a billion dollars. That means they were about eight thousand times wealthier than the typical high-income family in 1983. A billionaire is a thousand times richer than a mere millionaire.

According to *Forbes* magazine, about 40% of the richest 400 people of 1985 made their own fortunes. For instance, Sam Moore Walton, the richest man of that year, started with very little and founded a successful chain of retail stores.

But about 45% control fortunes that were mostly or entirely inherited, like the Hunt sisters pictured here. The other 15% had a significant inheritance that helped them get started.

SEE ALSO 1.6

1.3 ☐ WHO GETS INCOME FROM PROPERTY?

▲▲

A lot of folks get a little bit of income from property—54% of all adults in 1983, to be exact. But very few individuals—only 2%—got more than $10,000. This income came from such sources as interest, rents, dividends from stock, or sale of real estate or stock.

People who take in less than $50,000 a year get most of their money from work rather than from property. A 1982 survey of federal tax returns showed that only 10% of the taxable income of this group came from property.

Some very rich people earn high salaries at their jobs. But they often don't need it. Only about 30% of the income of individuals with taxable incomes over $500,000 in 1982 came from work. The remaining 70% came from property.

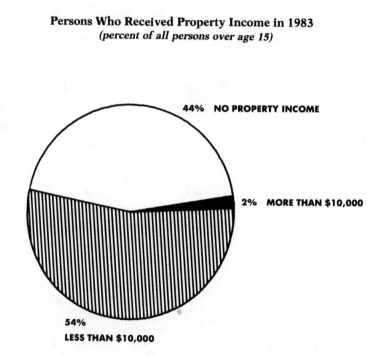

Persons Who Received Property Income in 1983
(percent of all persons over age 15)

44%   NO PROPERTY INCOME

2%   MORE THAN $10,000

54%
LESS THAN $10,000

1.4 ☐ WHAT DO THE WEALTHY OWN?

In 1983, according to a financial survey by the Federal Reserve Bank:

▲▲▲ The top 2% of income recipients owned 50% of all stocks and 39% of all bonds.

▲▲▲ The top 2% of all wealth holders owned 54% of all net financial assets. More than half of all families either had no financial assets or owed more than they owned.

▲▲▲ Only 19% of all families in the U.S. owned stocks, and only 3% owned bonds.

▲▲

*M*oney talks, and its political voice is getting louder every year. Increases in campaign contributions from political action committees (PACs) have bid up the price of political influence.

In 1984, senators who won closely contested races spent an average of $6.5 million on their campaigns, far more than was spent in comparable campaigns in 1974. And that's just the average. In 1984, Republican senator Jesse Helms of North Carolina spent a record $16.5 million to defeat Democrat James Hunt, who spent $9.5 million.

A 1980 survey showed that less than 7% of the population made direct campaign contributions to political candidates. Since most of these are very small, the big ones have a big impact.

Campaign Spending by Winning Senators in Closely Contested Races
(average millions spent in $1985, where winner won by 55% or less)

THE DOLLAR VOTES COME IN
LONG BEFORE THE BALLOT BOXES OPEN

6.7

1.1 1.6

1974   1980   1984

Because money can buy control over corporate decisions, the very wealthy wield a lot of influence over the U.S. economy. Just how much influence is difficult to say.

But if we make two assumptions, we can easily estimate how much control they could exercise. First, individuals can borrow an amount of money equivalent to their assets. Second, because a corporation's stock is usually divided among many shareholders, any one who owns 15% of the total stock of a company can pretty well control management decisions.

Applying those assumptions, we can suppose that the richest 400 people and 77 families of 1984 could have controlled about 42% of all the privately owned factories and equipment in the U.S.

▲▲▲ In 1984, the richest 400 people and 77 families directly owned assets worth about $181 billion.

▲▲▲ If they borrowed an equal amount, they could invest $362 billion dollars.

▲▲▲ If they bought 15% of the stock of as many large corporations as possible, they could then control about $2.4 trillion of productive assets.

▲▲▲ That sum amounts to about 42% of the privately owned factories and equipment in the U.S.

1.7 □ LARGE FIRMS DOMINATE MANY INDUSTRIES

▲▲▲▲▲▲▲▲▲▲▲▲▲▲▲▲▲▲▲▲▲▲▲▲▲▲▲▲▲▲▲▲▲▲▲▲▲▲▲

*T*ew U.S. corporations play monopoly, but many are part of a more complicated game called oligopoly, where several large firms, rather than just one, dominate an industry.

In 1985, the largest firms accounted for a very large percentage of total production in major industries such as aircraft and computer equipment. These firms can't raise prices on a whim, partly because of international competition. But they can easily work together to defend their interests.

For instance, truly competitive bidding for military aircraft can never take place, because Boeing, McDonnell-Douglas, and Lockheed dominate the industry. And no matter how many small computer companies challenge IBM, few if any will be able to outlast the huge firm that sets the technological standard for the industry.

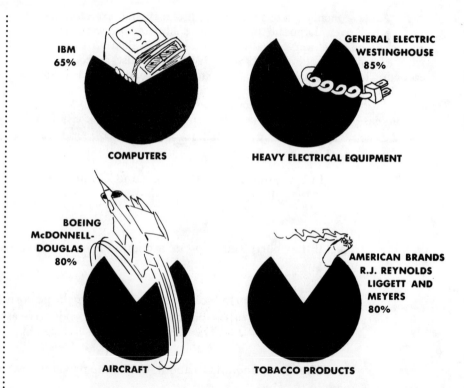

IBM
65%

COMPUTERS

GENERAL ELECTRIC
WESTINGHOUSE
85%

HEAVY ELECTRICAL EQUIPMENT

BOEING
McDONNELL-
DOUGLAS
80%

AIRCRAFT

AMERICAN BRANDS
R.J. REYNOLDS
LIGGETT AND
MEYERS
80%

TOBACCO PRODUCTS

Assets Owned by the Top 100 Industrial Firms
(percent of total assets of nonfinancial corporations)

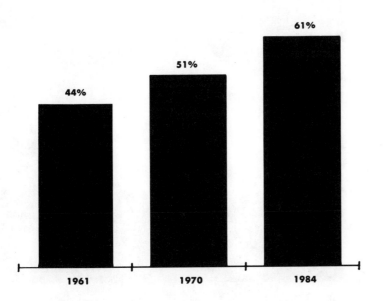

As names like United Brands imply, many U.S. firms are engaged in more than one line of business: they are conglomerates. Their economic power can't be gauged by their share of any one industry, but comparing their assets to total corporate assets reveals a great concentration of economic power.

By this measure, the top 100 industrial corporations in the U.S. have substantially increased their influence. Their combined assets amounted to 61% of total assets of nonfinancial corporations in 1984, compared to 44% in 1961. Nonfinancial corporations include all corporations except banks.

On the other hand, foreign competition has diminished the economic power of many large U.S. firms, and new, relatively small businesses in the growing service sector help counterbalance the old industrial giants.

1.9 ☐ MORE MONEY FOR MERGERS

▲▲

*I*n 1984 and 1985, U.S. corporations began gobbling each other up in a wave of mergers and acquisitions that increased the power and influence of large firms. The relaxation of traditional standards of antitrust law contributed to this trend.

Antitrust laws were originally designed to maintain competition and to protect small businesses. Under the Reagan administration, however, the Justice Department has argued that diminished competition is acceptable if it increases economic efficiency.

But large mergers don't always make better companies, and merger mania has proved costly. To avoid takeover, some companies swallowed "poison pills"—loads of debt—to make themselves less attractive to potential buyers. And the wave of takeovers helped raise corporate debt to unprecedented levels.

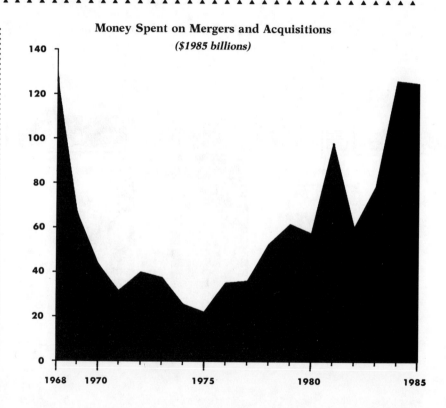

Money Spent on Mergers and Acquisitions
($1985 billions)

1.10 □ THE BIGGEST MERGERS OF 1985

▲▲▲

VALUE (billions)	BUYER	COMPANY BOUGHT
$6.3	General Electric	RCA
$6.2	Kohlberg, Kravis, Roberts	Beatrice
$5.8	Phillip Morris	General Foods
$5.1	General Motors	Hughes Aircraft
$5.0	Allied Corporation	Signal Companies
$4.9	R.J. Reynolds	Nabisco
$3.8	Baxter Travenol	American Hospital Supply
$3.7	U.S. Steel	Texas Oil and Gas

The huge sums involved in mergers in 1985 brought enormous windfall gains to stockholders but did little to increase the productive capacity of the economy. Money spent acquiring another company is money that could have been invested in new facilities and equipment.

The money spent on the eight largest mergers amounted to almost $41 billion. Compare that sum to the total amount of money devoted to new investment in the productive capacity of the economy in 1985: $133 billion. The money that changed hands in those eight mergers could have increased productive investment by 30%.

▲ ▲

There are almost as many banks in this country as there are Main Streets. But many of them are being overshadowed by banks of the sky scraper variety.

Until recently, restrictions on interstate banking, as well as interest ceilings, made it easier for small local banks to survive. Deregulation eliminated some of these restrictions and provided some important benefits to consumers. For instance, interest rates on savings accounts increased as banks competed with one another for deposits.

But deregulation has increased the financial pressures on small banks and contributed to economic concentration.

In 1983 the top ten commercial banks held 34% of all bank assets. If one of them went under, Main Streets all across the country would be shaken.

The Distribution of Bank Assets in 1983

THE TOP 0.1% OF ALL COMMERCIAL BANKS (10 OUT OF 14,500):

HELD 34% OF ALL BANK ASSETS

Bank of America

Citicorp

Chase Manhattan

Manufacturers Hanover

J.P. Morgan

First Interstate

Continental Illinois

Chemical N.Y.

First Chicago

Security Pacific

1.12 ☐ THE SIZE OF MULTINATIONAL ENTERPRISE

▲▲

Most of the largest corporations in the world have operations in more than one country and are often called multinationals. Ability to move in and out of different countries gives corporations considerable bargaining power in their dealings with local employees and host countries.

The sheer size of many multinational enterprises makes them difficult to regulate. They are almost nations unto themselves. The worldwide sales of the three largest companies in the world in 1981 were far greater than the value of all goods sold (gross domestic product) in many small countries.

Worldwide Sales of the Three Largest Companies in the World in 1981
Gross Domestic Product of Some Developing Countries in 1981

$113 BILLION

$82 BILLION

$69 BILLION

$4.7 BILLION $35 BILLION

$2.7 BILLION

NICARAGUA   ZIMBABWE   PHILIPPINES   MOBIL   SHELL   EXXON

SEE ALSO 10.9

1.13 □ WORKERS AS OWNERS

▲▲

orker ownership is one alternative to the current concentration of wealth in the U.S. economy. Many people can buy shares in the companies they work for through Employee Stock-Ownership Plans (ESOPs). In recent years, changes in tax laws have made the plans very popular. In 1985, more than 7 million workers, representing more than 6% of all employed workers, belonged to some form of ESOP.

The notion that stock ownership automatically gives workers control over their jobs is an ESOPs fable. The stock shares are commonly held in trust for the employees by a bank or other institution, so most workers share the risk of ownership without enjoying any real control.

Still, some ESOPs encourage worker participation and try to break down the conventional distinction between owners and workers.

Number of Employees Enrolled in Employee Stock-Ownership Plans
(millions)

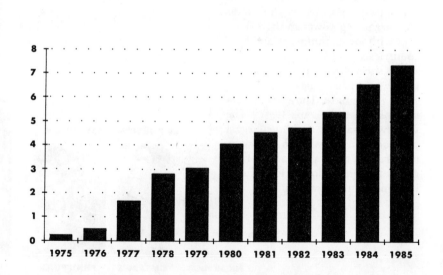

In 1985, the total assets of corporate, state, and local employee-benefit funds amounted to over $1.3 trillion.

Much of this money was invested in corporate stocks and bonds. According to one recent estimate, about 23% of all corporate stocks and about 50% of all corporate bonds were held by pension funds in 1984.

The General Motors Corporation controls the largest corporate employee-benefit plan in the country. In 1985, its assets were worth $22.9 billion.

Workers seldom have any control over how their pension funds are invested or what kinds of companies they are invested in. If they gained some control over this "social capital," they could change the face of corporate America.

What kinds of work do people do? How much do they get paid? How many people are unemployed, and why? What's happened to unions? This chapter traces the answers to these four questions over the last thirty-five years.

More women are working nine-to-five. As Chart 2.1 shows, women have entered the labor force in greater numbers than men in recent years. There have also been some major changes in the types of work people do. Service-sector jobs were widespread back in 1950, but as Chart 2.2 illustrates, they now account for about 70% of all jobs. Since 1980, the decline in the percent-age of manufacturing jobs within the entire economy has been particularly steep, while employment in personal and business services has ballooned (see Charts 2.3 and 2.4).

Once upon a time, workers could look forward to wage increases every year. Chart 2.5 tracks the steady growth in hourly earnings, corrected for inflation, between 1950 and 1974. Since that year, earnings have gone down overall, increasing only slightly in 1986. A look at trends in weekly earnings by race and sex in Chart 2.6 shows that women fared better than men in the early 1980s, probably because they were less concentrated in the hard-hit manufacturing sector.

Workers at the bottom of the pay scale suffered a particularly big cut in their buying power in the 1970s and 1980s. Chart 2.7 shows that increases in the federal minimum wage were not sufficient to compensate for inflation after about 1970. Of course, pay is not the only aspect of employee compensation. In the 1970s, employer contributions to pension plans and health insurance (especially for well-paid workers) became far more common. By 1985 they accounted for about 13% of an average employer's total payroll costs, and legally required payments such as Social Security accounted for another 9%. But as Chart 2.8 demonstrates, the era of increasing worker benefits seems to be ending.

The kinds of jobs people do and the wages they receive shape everyday life. But when people can't find a job, their everyday life can fall apart. In 1986, unemployment averaged 7%, and was far higher for some groups. Chart 2.9 shows that 15% of all blacks and 18% of people aged 16 to 19 were unemployed. Furthermore, the official unemployment rate understates the actual percentage of people who wanted work but couldn't find it. Chart 2.10 explains that the true unemployment rate in 1986 was over 10%.

Unemployment is on the increase. Although employment trends are always marked by zigs and zags, Chart 2.11 reveals a definite upward trend. Other countries, such as Great Britain and West Germany, have also suffered increased unemployment. But as Chart 2.12 shows, Japan and Sweden have managed to keep their unemployment rates relatively low, partly by making that a political priority.

The unemployment problem in this country can't be explained away as a result of more women looking for jobs. The fastest growing category of the unemployed are job losers—people fired or laid off from their jobs (see Chart 2.13). And a large share of those people were displaced by major plant closings. As Chart 2.14 shows, these workers suffer long-lasting ill effects.

Historically, trade unions have served as a powerful tool for increasing the living standards of their members and, to some extent, those of workers in general. Unions still represent almost one out of five U.S. workers; men, blacks, and workers in manufacturing, transportation, and government are most likely to belong to a union (see Chart 2.15). But as Chart 2.16 demonstrates, union membership has been falling since the 1950s.

Chart 2.17 helps explain the problems unions face. Despite higher wages and better working conditions than non-union counterparts, union members haven't increased their real wages in recent years. High unemployment rates and reduced social spending have increased the cost of losing a job, as shown in Chart 2.18. Workers just don't have much bargaining power in a sluggish economy.

2.1 □ MEN AND WOMEN IN THE LABOR FORCE

▲▲▲

The labor force has expanded in recent years as more women have entered it. Of course, women have always worked, but those who perform household labor aren't officially considered part of the labor force. Only paid workers or people looking for paid work are counted.

The number of men in the labor force has remained relatively constant because their labor-force participation rate (the percentage of men over age 16 working or seeking work) has declined enough to counterbalance population growth.

Expanding Social Security benefits have led to earlier retirement for many men. And many black men, discouraged by persistently high levels of unemployment, have stopped looking for work.

Also, men may be more likely than women to get paid off the books, outside the official labor force, in the underground economy.

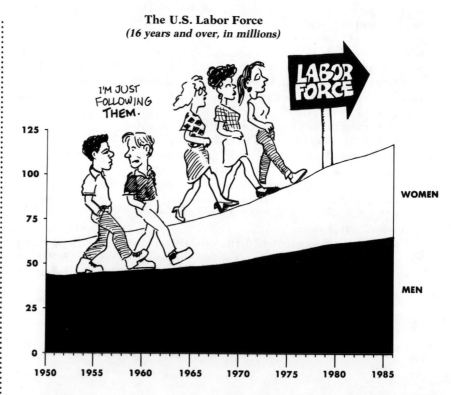

The U.S. Labor Force
(16 years and over, in millions)

SEE ALSO 3.1

The Changing Industrial Composition of Employment

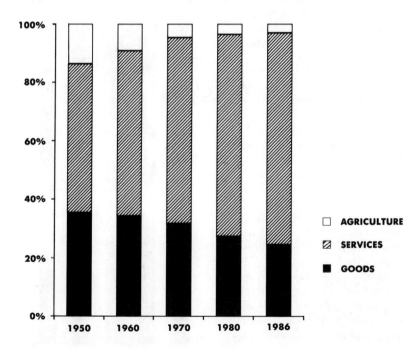

□ AGRICULTURE
▨ SERVICES
■ GOODS

*M*ost workers today provide services rather than produce a product. The term "services" is a catchall category for very diverse economic activities that usually involve transactions with people or information.

As early as 1950, more than half the labor force worked in service jobs. Since then, the percentage has increased to about 70%.

Employment in agriculture, forestry, and fisheries has continued a steady decline that began at the turn of the century and quickened after 1950. By 1986, only 3% of the labor force worked on the land.

The share of the labor force in manufacturing, mining, and construction began to decline slowly after 1960, when it accounted for 34% of the total. By 1980, it had fallen to 30%. Between 1980 and 1986, the percentage dropped to 25%.

This steep decline was largely due to increased imports replacing goods made by U.S. workers.

2.3 ☐ FEWER MANUFACTURING JOBS

▲ ▲

Manufacturing jobs, historically better paid than most service jobs, are getting scarce.

The share of employment in the production of nondurable goods (those with a short life span, such as textiles, leather, and paper) began

to decline about 1960. The share of employment in durable goods (those that last a long time, such as steel and autos) began to decline after 1970 and dropped very rapidly between 1980 and 1986.

Over those six years the total number of manufacturing jobs, rather than just their percentage of all jobs, declined. About a million manufacturing jobs disappeared.

Part of the explanation lies in new international trends. Imported textiles, shoes, electronic components, and autos now account for a large share of U.S. consumption. And many U.S. manufacturing firms have moved their operations abroad to take advantage of cheaper labor and less regulation.

Automation also played a role. The average price of an industrial robot fell 20% between 1984 and 1985, making these "steel-collar" workers particularly attractive to employers.

Employment in Manufacturing as a Percentage of Total Employment

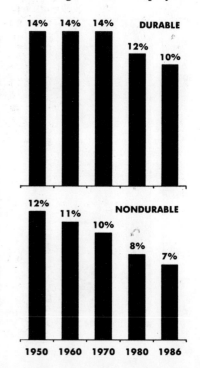

SEE ALSO 10.6

▲▲

Employment in Service Industries as a Percentage of Total Employment

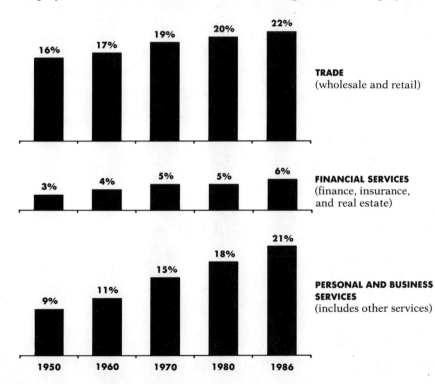

TRADE
(wholesale and retail)

FINANCIAL SERVICES
(finance, insurance,
and real estate)

**PERSONAL AND BUSINESS
SERVICES**
(includes other services)

*M*ost service jobs fall into the category of trade, financial, or personal and business services. These service jobs accounted for almost half of all jobs in the U.S. in 1986. Trade alone accounted for more than 20% of all employment (slightly more than the 17% employed in manufacturing).

Why have service jobs expanded so rapidly? One reason is that it is harder to substitute machines for people in services than in manufacturing.

Another important factor is the decline in household production. Wage earners spend considerable money buying substitutes for services provided at home. In 1984, for instance, about 30% of all money spent on food was spent in eating and drinking establishments compared to about 21% in 1950.

Most workers began to feel a pay pinch in the mid-1970s. Real average hourly earnings had increased steadily since 1950. But after 1974, they were squeezed.

Inflation was the initial cause of the pinch—wages simply didn't keep up with sudden price increases in 1974 and 1979. But even when inflation abated in the 1980s, real earnings remained stagnant. In 1986, the average hourly wage, at $8.60, was lower than it had been in 1967, at $8.63 (in 1985 dollars).

Spendable earnings, or take-home pay, fell at an even faster rate, partly because of increases in Social Security taxes. In 1981 (the latest year for which the data are available), the average worker took home less hourly pay than in 1964.

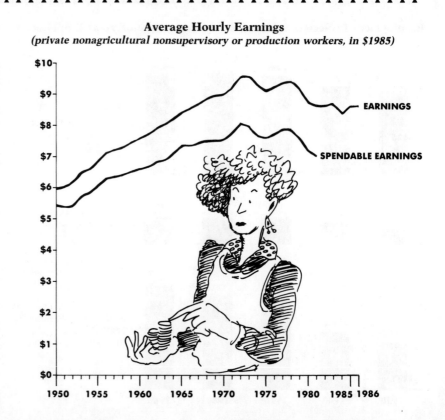

Average Hourly Earnings
(private nonagricultural nonsupervisory or production workers, in $1985)

EARNINGS

SPENDABLE EARNINGS

$10 $9 $8 $7 $6 $5 $4 $3 $2 $1 $0

1950 1955 1960 1965 1970 1975 1980 1985 1986

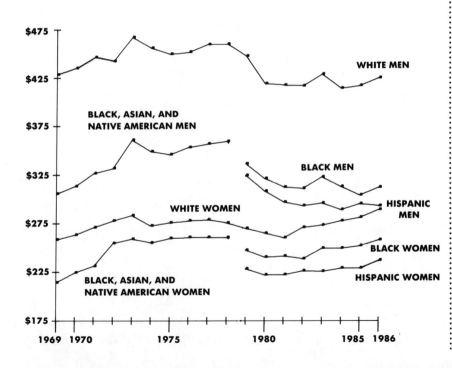

Median Weekly Earnings of Full-Time Workers
($1985)

WHITE MEN

BLACK, ASIAN, AND NATIVE AMERICAN MEN

BLACK MEN

WHITE WOMEN

HISPANIC MEN

BLACK WOMEN

BLACK, ASIAN, AND NATIVE AMERICAN WOMEN

HISPANIC WOMEN

$475
$425
$375
$325
$275
$225
$175

1969 1970   1975   1980   1985 1986

Like real hourly wages, real weekly earnings tended downward after about 1973. But men experienced steeper declines than women from 1973 to 1975 and from 1978 to 1980; since 1981, women's weekly earnings have increased. Whatever their gender, whites fared better than people of color.

In 1979, the Census Bureau began to publish distinct statistics for blacks rather than for the larger category of all minority groups. As a result, changes between 1978 and 1979 can't be accurately assessed. After 1979, weekly earnings of black men and Hispanic men declined steadily, while those of white men stayed level.

Women were less likely than men to be employed in hard-hit manufacturing jobs. Affirmative action also worked to their advantage. In 1986, a typical white woman, working full-time, actually earned more per week than she did in 1973.

▲▲

The real minimum wage in 1986 was lower than it was in 1950, the year it was first established by law at $0.75 an hour. Converted to 1985 dollars, that $0.75 amounts to $3.35, the legal minimum since 1981.

In the 1950s and 1960s, the minimum wage was boosted several times, more than enough to compensate for inflation. In 1968, it reached almost $5.00 an hour (in 1985 dollars). Since then, it has been allowed to decline.

The low minimum wage means poverty for many families. At $3.35 an hour in 1985, a full-time worker brought home less than $7,000 a year, far below the poverty level established by the Census Bureau for a family of four (about $11,000).

Some economists argue that the minimum wage discourages employers from hiring young workers. But youth unemployment increased in the 1980s despite declines in real minimum wages.

Real Minimum Wage
($1985)

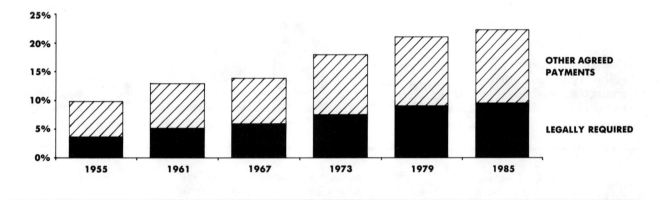

Average Benefit Costs as a Percentage of Employer's Total Payroll Costs

OTHER AGREED PAYMENTS

LEGALLY REQUIRED

People depend on more than the take-home pay in their paycheck. In today's economy, benefits are an important part of employee compensation. Employers' contributions to legally required payments such as Social Security and to other agreed payments such as health insurance increased dramatically as a percentage of their total payroll costs throughout the 1960s and early 1970s. But in recent years, that percentage has risen only slightly.

According to an annual U.S. Chamber of Commerce survey of about 1,500 employers, benefits for hourly rated employees increased from about 10% of total payroll costs in 1955 to 22% in 1985.

Apart from those required by law, benefits vary widely among companies. Large firms tend to provide more benefits than small firms, especially in the manufacturing sector.

Individuals Seeking Work as a Percentage of the Labor Force in 1986

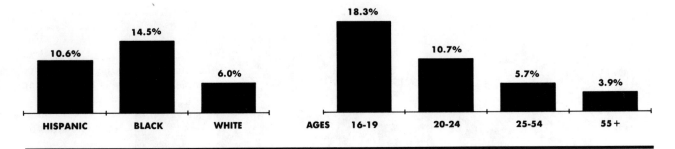

Some groups of workers are far more prone to unemployment than others. In 1986, the average unemployment rate was 7%, but unemployment rates for blacks and Hispanics were far higher, at 14.5% and 10.6%, respectively.

Young people are also especially vulnerable to unemployment. Even for those between 20 and 25 the unemployment rate was far above the average.

The annual unemployment rate is an average of unemployment rates in different months. Because there is considerable turnover, the number of people who experience a spell of unemployment over the course of a year is more than two and a half times the number unemployed in any given month. More than 17% of the labor force experienced some unemployment in 1985.

Workers qualify for unemployment benefits only if they have been fired or laid-off. And benefits normally last a maximum of six months. Only about half the unemployed receive them.

Unemployment is hard on people. Statistical studies show that it leads to increases in such problems as alcoholism, child abuse, and mental illness.

SEE ALSO 4.7, 4.8

▲ ▲

*P*eople aren't counted among the unemployed unless they are able and willing to work and actively seeking employment. The unemployment rate is the number of unemployed divided by the number in the labor force (people working plus those seeking work), expressed as a percentage.

The unemployment rate understates the percentage of workers without jobs.

In 1986, although the unemployment rate was 7%:

▲▲▲ 1,121,000 individuals wanted a job but had given up looking for one. If those discouraged workers had been counted among the unemployed, the rate would have been 7.9%.

▲▲▲ Another 5,588,000 individuals were working part-time but wanted full-time jobs—in other words, they had about half as much employment as they needed. So, if half of these were also counted among the unemployed, the rate would have been 10.3%.

2.11 □ THE INCREASE IN UNEMPLOYMENT

▲▲

*U*nemployment rates move like a roller coaster, going up when economic growth slows, back down again when economic growth picks up. But overall in the past fifteen years, the roller coaster has been heading up.

Until about 1974, unemployment was generally below 5%. Since then, however, slow economic growth kept the unemployment rate consistently above that level. In both 1984 and 1985, years of economic recovery, unemployment was expected to decline. Instead it remained above 7%, far higher than the unemployment rate of earlier recession years.

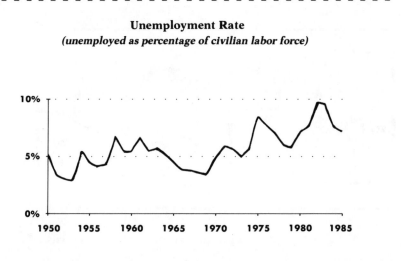

Unemployment Rate
(unemployed as percentage of civilian labor force)

SEE ALSO 9.2

▲▲

Unemployment Trends in Major Industrial Economies
(adjusted to approximate U.S. definitions)

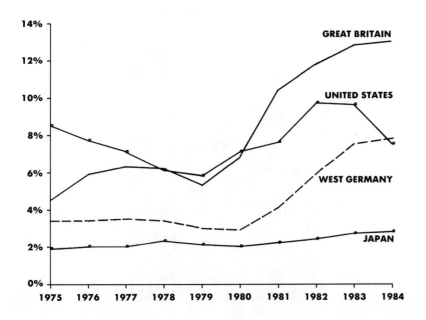

*U*S. workers are more likely to be unemployed than most of their counterparts in other advanced capitalist countries. Why? The rate of economic growth is one important factor.

West Germany and Japan enjoyed faster growth than the U.S. in the 1970s and therefore had more jobs to go around. In 1983 and 1984, the U.S. economy grew faster than either of those countries. As a result, unemployment dropped to the level of West Germany's rate.

Public policy also plays an important role. Unlike the U.S., most European countries, as well as Japan, have strong public policies designed to lower unemployment, such as retraining and job-referral programs. Sweden has maintained relatively low unemployment rates despite its relatively slow economic growth.

▲ ▲

*P*eople end up in un-employment lines for different reasons. Some are new entrants into the labor market, such as young people who have just left school, or re-entrants, such as woman who have taken time out to rear children; others are job leavers who have voluntarily left their jobs, or job losers, those laid off or fired.

Some people argue that increased unemployment rates simply reflect the large size of the baby-boom generation. But by far the fastest-growing group of unemployed are job losers—more than 50% of the unemployed in 1984. In recession years, the relative number of job losers tends to increase, but in the 1980s, their share of total unemployment has been higher, even in years of economic expansion.

The increased unemployment of the 1980s reflects widespread layoffs which have left many industrial workers with very poor job prospects.

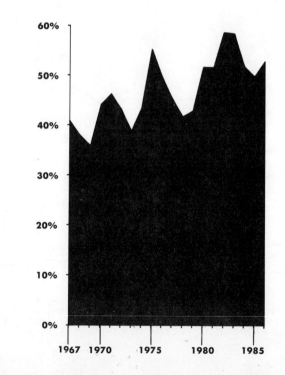

Job Losers as a Percentage of the Unemployed
(job losers relative to job leavers, new entrants , and reentrants)

SEE ALSO 2.18

▲▲▲▲▲▲▲▲▲▲▲▲▲▲▲▲▲▲▲▲▲▲▲▲▲

▲▲▲ Between January 1975 and January 1984, 11.5 million workers (over 10% of all U.S. workers) were fired or laid off because of plant closings or employment cutbacks.

▲▲▲ A Bureau of Labor Statistics survey focusing on the 5.1 million of these workers who had worked at least three years at their job found that:

—about 3.1 million, or 60%, of these workers were reemployed by January 1984, but about half those were earning less than they had in their previous jobs.

—about 1.3 million, or 25% of these workers were still looking for work in January 1984 (the other 15% left the labor force).

—many workers exhausted their unemployment insurance, and of the 1.3 million workers who remained jobless, only 40% had any health insurance at the time of the survey.

2.15 ☐ WHO BELONGS TO UNIONS?

▲▲

*A*bout 18% of U.S. employees belonged to unions in 1986. The likelihood of being a union member varied considerably by a worker's race and gender, and by the type of industry he or she worked in.

More than 22% of all employed men were union members, as opposed to 13% of all employed women. A much higher percentage of blacks (24%) than either whites (17%) or Hispanics (18%) were represented by unions.

Although a relatively large portion of workers in manufacturing and transportation were represented by unions, government workers had the highest representation, including teachers and protective-service workers (such as police officers).

The overall level of unionization is higher in Japan, at about 30% of all employees, and even higher in most European countries, at between 40% and 50%.

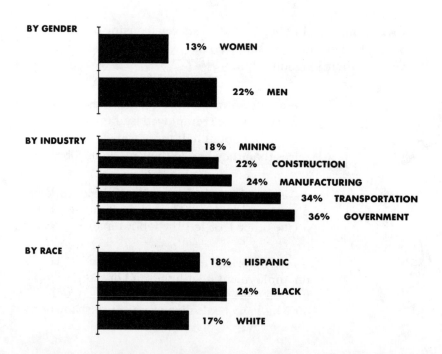

Percentage of All Employees in Various Groups Belonging to Unions in 1986

BY GENDER
- 13% WOMEN
- 22% MEN

BY INDUSTRY
- 18% MINING
- 22% CONSTRUCTION
- 24% MANUFACTURING
- 34% TRANSPORTATION
- 36% GOVERNMENT

BY RACE
- 18% HISPANIC
- 24% BLACK
- 17% WHITE

Unionized Employees
(through 1978, as percentage of nonagricultural workers; 1980 and after, as percentage of all employees)

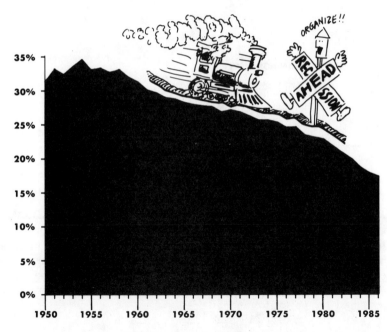

US. workers are far less likely to carry a union card these days. The number of union members has declined steadily as a percentage of all nonagricultural employees, from about 35% in 1954 to 24% in 1978.

Though more recent figures are not strictly comparable, they reveal an even more rapid rate of decline. Unions represented 23% of all employees in 1980 but only 18% in 1986.

Until 1980, unions grew in membership despite a decrease in their percentage share. But between 1980 and 1984, they lost 2.7 million members, partly because the recession of 1981 and 1982 led to job losses.

But there are other reasons for the decline. Employers' resistance to unionization has grown—and with it the number of worker complaints of unfair labor practices (such as firing union organizers), which more than doubled beteen 1970 and 1980.

Union members still enjoy higher wages than non-union workers in comparable jobs. And until about 1974, union wage gains consistently outpaced increases in the consumer price index.

After 1974, however, union members began to lose out against inflation. Cost-of-living agreements (COLAs) in labor contracts offered them some protection in the mid-1970s, but in the late 1970s and early 1980s increases in consumer prices were higher than union wage increases.

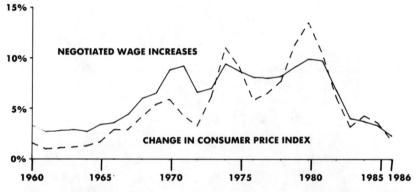

Median Union Wage Increases Relative to Inflation
(nonsupervisory employees in nonfarm private sector)

NEGOTIATED WAGE INCREASES

CHANGE IN CONSUMER PRICE INDEX

SOUNDS LIKE THE FIZZ IS GONE

Unfavorable political circumstances and high unemployment rates have diminished strike activity in recent years. Unions simply haven't had the power to demand higher wages. As a result, most unionized workers, like their non-unionized counterparts, have seen their real wages. stagnate or decline.

2.18 □ THE COST OF JOB LOSS

▲▲

What's the cost of losing a job? The answer depends on what is happening in the economy as whole, as well as on personal circumstances. Two factors are particularly important: the overall unemployment rate, which affects the average length of time it takes to find a new job; and the kinds of public assistance, such as unemployment benefits or food stamps, that can be relied on in the meantime.

Considering those factors, it's possible to estimate the cost of job loss as a percentage of the average

worker's expected standard of living. The cost of job loss dropped in the 1960s because low unemployment rates made it easier for people to find new jobs. The expansion of social programs also helped the unemployed.

In the 1970s, however, unemployment rates increased. Then, in the early 1980s, cuts in social programs also kicked up the cost of job loss.

The higher the cost of job loss, the more threatening unemployment is. And the greater the threat of unemployment, the less likely workers are to complain about wages and working conditions.

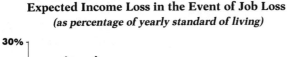

Expected Income Loss in the Event of Job Loss
(as percentage of yearly standard of living)

"You haven't come a long way, baby." Imagine the woman's gentle voice, as the camera focuses on a flattering angle of a man struggling to use a vacuum cleaner. You probably won't see it on television, but it would be a good antidote to the ads you do see. And it's a reminder that both men and women have a long way to go to achieve an economy with a fair division of labor between the sexes.

How has women's place in the economy changed in recent years? As Chart 3.1 shows, more and more women, especially mothers, have entered the wage labor force. But women still do most of the housework.

Chart 3.2 summarizes a study that suggests that the time women spend on housework has not diminished enough to compensate for the extra time they now devote to wage work.

Women's traditional household responsibilities have always influenced the types of paid work they were allowed or encouraged to undertake. In recent years many women have moved into well-paying professional jobs once monopolized by men, as seen in Chart 3.3. On the other hand, as Chart 3.4 points out, most women remain in sex-typed and low-paying pink-collar jobs.

Women have narrowed the gender wage gap. Chart 3.5 documents substantial improvements in the relative earnings of full-time women wage earners, while Chart 3.6 shows that young women have made particularly dramatic gains in the 1980s. Still, women stuck in traditionally female jobs tend to be paid less than men doing work of comparable worth. Chart 3.7 provides some typical comparisons. Unless the new concern with pay equity takes hold, inequality between men's and women's wages in the U.S. could remain high by international standards. As Chart 3.8 shows, women fare better relative to men in Australia and West Germany; Japan is one of the few major industrialized countries with even greater wage inequality between the sexes than the U.S.

Have women's higher wages been counterbalanced by new family problems? Married-couple families still make up a majority of U.S. households. But as Chart 3.9 shows, their majority is shrinking. Women maintain a growing percentage of all households; they maintain an even faster growing percentage of all families with one or more children under 18, as documented in Chart 3.10. This demographic shift has been accompanied by two economic trends: First, as Chart 3.11 shows, many fathers fail to contribute adequately to the support of their children. Second, as Chart 3.12 shows, public assistance for women with dependent children has declined.

As a result of these demographic and economic trends, women's income relative to men's has probably declined over the past fifteen years. Chart 3.13 explains the assumptions behind such an estimate. Women with children are certainly more likely to live in poverty than they were in 1959. As Chart 3.14 shows, families maintained by women alone now make up almost half of all families living below the poverty line.

Women bear a disproportionate share of the economic costs and risks of rearing children. Yet their ability to make their own decisions about childbearing is limited in a number of ways, as described in Chart 3.15. Many working women who want children can't get maternity leave from their employers, and as Chart 3.16 suggests, high-quality day care should become a social priority.

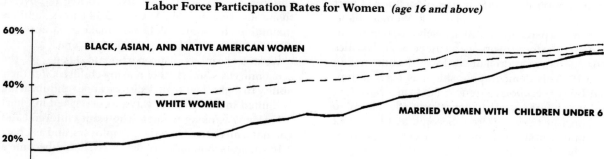

Labor Force Participation Rates for Women *(age 16 and above)*

BLACK, ASIAN, AND NATIVE AMERICAN WOMEN

WHITE WOMEN

MARRIED WOMEN WITH CHILDREN UNDER 6

*E*very year, more women bring home a paycheck. Since the 1850s, women's work has steadily shifted from the home to the factory, shop, and office. Since the late 1970s more than 50% of women over age 16 have been working or looking for work in the paid labor force.

Black women have long been more likely than other women to work for pay, largely because of the legacy of slavery and discrimination. Today, however, there is little difference in the labor-force participation of women by race, because white women have entered the labor force at a particularly rapid rate in recent years.

Mothers are the fastest growing group within the labor force. By 1986, 54% of married women with children under 6 were in the labor force, although only about 25% worked full time.

SEE ALSO 2.1

3.2 ☐ WOMEN STILL DO MOST OF THE HOUSEWORK

Average Hours of Housework Per Week

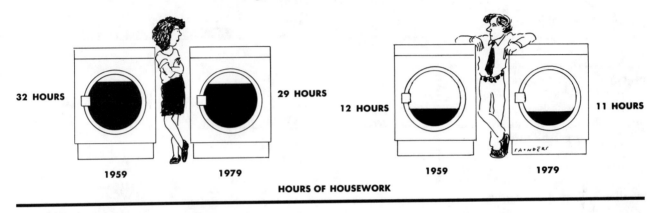

32 HOURS   **29 HOURS**   **12 HOURS**   **11 HOURS**

1959   1979   1959   1979

HOURS OF HOUSEWORK

A woman's work is never done. In fact, there may be more of it than ever. Despite their increasing participation in the labor force, women still do far more housework than men—in 1979, about 29 hours per week, compared to 11 hours for men.

In 1979, as in 1959, women put in about 73% of all the time devoted to housework. The average woman added 6 hours per week to time spent on paid work between 1959 and 1979, but decreased her household work by only 3 hours.

Men, on the other hand, decreased both the time spent per week on paid work (by 2 hours) and on housework (by 1 hour).

Other studies show that when a baby is added to the household, women's work time at home skyrockets, while men's usually remains about the same.

Time-budget studies have been performed only in a relatively small number of households and thus are not terribly reliable. If more economists did housework, more data would probably be available.

More women are getting higher-paying professional jobs. In the 1950s and 1960s women were often discouraged from entering professions such as engineering and medicine. But in the 1970s, a militant women's movement helped women gain access to traditionally male jobs. Affirmative-action programs were particularly successful at improving women's opportunities to pursue professional training.

By 1986, women accounted for 7% of all engineers, 16% of all doctors, 17% of all lawyers and judges, and 38% of all managers.

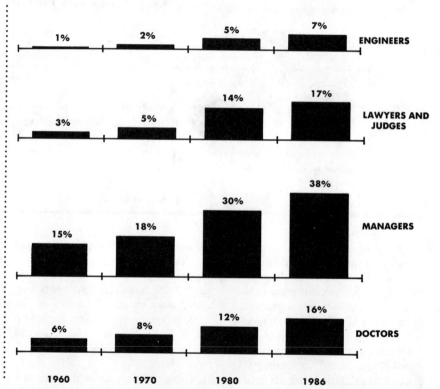

ENGINEERS
1% 2% 5% 7%

LAWYERS AND JUDGES
3% 5% 14% 17%

MANAGERS
15% 18% 30% 38%

DOCTORS
6% 8% 12% 16%

1960 1970 1980 1986

3.4 □ PINK-COLLAR JOBS

▲▲▲

*W*hile some women have entered traditionally male fields, most still work in "women's jobs." In 1986, 62% of all working women were employed in occupations in which at least 70% of all employees were female.

Many of these occupations are just as "pink-collar" as they were over twenty years ago. For instance, 97% of all secretaries, stenographers, and typists in 1986 were women—exactly the same percentage as in 1960. The percentage of teachers who were women also remained unchanged.

Occupational segregation puts women at an economic disadvantage. The greater the number of women relative to men in an occupation, the lower the average pay.

Women Employed in Occupations at least 70% Female in 1986
(as percentage of all women employed)

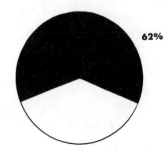

62%

*I*n 1986, women working full time earned about sixty-nine cents for every dollar earned by their male counterparts. The difference between women's and men's wages was greatest among whites, with women earning 68% of what men earn, and least among blacks, at 83%, with Hispanics at 81%.

Between 1967 and 1979, white women's earnings seemed stuck at close to 60% of white men's, and no other groups of women enjoyed big relative gains. Then, between 1979 and 1986, all women earners gained on men.

Women entered better-paying jobs in the 1970s, but it took a while for them to reach the higher wage scales. Also, men's earnings failed to increase between 1979 and 1985. A very small increase in women's earnings was enough to reduce men's advantage further.

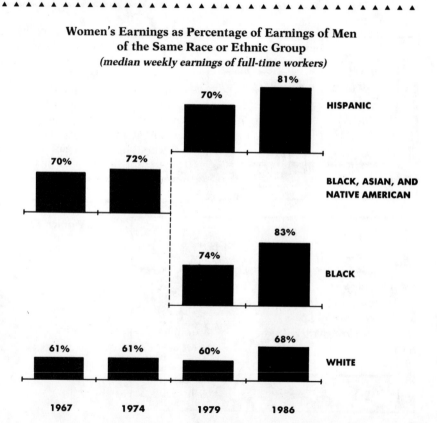

Women's Earnings as Percentage of Earnings of Men of the Same Race or Ethnic Group
(median weekly earnings of full-time workers)

HISPANIC — 70%, 81%

BLACK, ASIAN, AND NATIVE AMERICAN

70%, 72%

BLACK — 74%, 83%

WHITE — 61%, 61%, 60%, 68%

1967   1974   1979   1986

SEE ALSO 2.6

Earnings of Women, Ages 16–24 Relative to Men, Ages 16–24
(median weekly earnings of full-time workers)

Young women are giving young men a run for their money. Among workers aged 16 to 24, the earnings of women increased from 81% of those of men in 1980 to 89% in 1986.

The wide gap between the sexes tends to widen in mid-career, so it's hard to predict whether this new generation of women workers will maintain the gains they have made.

▲ ▲

*A*re women workers paid what they are worth? Jobs can be ranked into comparable categories according to their requirements (such as educational level) and characteristics (such as level of responsibility). Studies differ, but they usually show that women are paid far less than men for comparable jobs.

For instance, a registered nurse (usually a woman) requires as much education and takes as much responsibility as a vocational-education teacher (usually a man) but is usually paid far less.

In the 1980s, comparable worth, or pay equity, became a major issue for many states and municipalities, some of which faced lawsuits charging them with sex discrimination. Collective bargaining also convinced some (including the city of Los Angeles) to change relative pay scales. Some states, such as Iowa and Minnesota, are voluntarily implementing pay-equity policies.

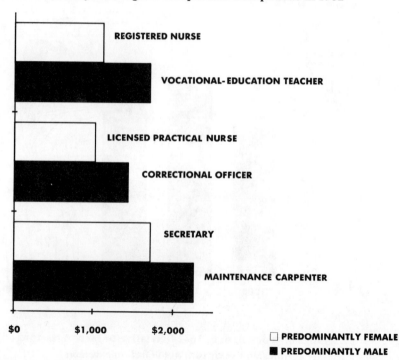

Monthly Earnings in Comparable Occupations in 1982

REGISTERED NURSE

VOCATIONAL-EDUCATION TEACHER

LICENSED PRACTICAL NURSE

CORRECTIONAL OFFICER

SECRETARY

MAINTENANCE CARPENTER

$0 $1,000 $2,000

□ PREDOMINANTLY FEMALE
■ PREDOMINANTLY MALE

Women's Wages as a Percentage of Men's Wages in 1985
(average hourly or median weekly earnings in nonagricultural employment)

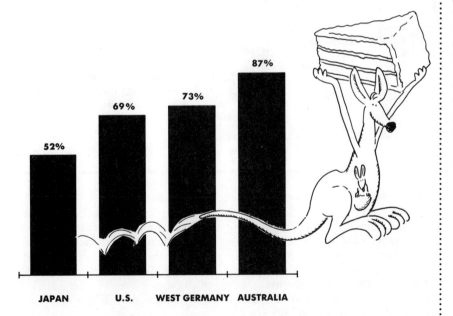

52% — JAPAN
69% — U.S.
73% — WEST GERMANY
87% — AUSTRALIA

*W*omen down under take the cake. In Australia, women earn more relative to men (87%) than in any other country reporting to the International Labour Organization in Geneva. One reason is the pay-equity policy adopted by the Australian government in the 1970s.

Women in many European countries fare slightly better than women in the U.S. In West Germany, for instance, women earn about 73% of what their male counterparts earn. In Japan, women earn only about 52% as much as men.

▲ ▲

The Changing Composition of Households

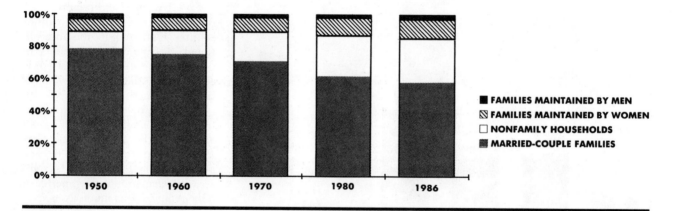

FAMILIES MAINTAINED BY MEN
FAMILIES MAINTAINED BY WOMEN
NONFAMILY HOUSEHOLDS
MARRIED-COUPLE FAMILIES

*M*om, Dad, Buddy, and Sue aren't as likely to live together as they once were. They may all have their own apartments. In 1950, almost 80% of all U.S. households were married-couple families. By 1985, less than 60% of households fit this description. And only about a third of these included children under 18.

More and more individuals, including the elderly, are choosing to live by themselves. Single-person households increased from 9% to 23% of all U.S. households between 1950 and 1986. The percentage of households that are families maintained by women also increased, from 8% to 12%.

Getting married is still popular. But the amount of time that men and women stay married has gone down as the divorce rate has risen. In 1983, only slightly more than 55% of all women over 15 were married and living with their husbands.

SEE ALSO T.5

Families with Children Maintained by Women
(as percentage of all families with one or more children under age 18)

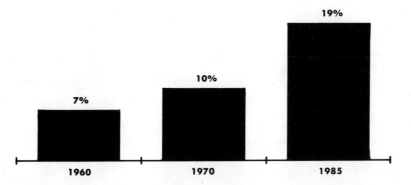

"No man present in the home" used to be the Census Bureau's definition of a female-headed household. But in 1980 the bureau dispensed with its traditional, authoritarian assumption that a household had to have a (male) head and substituted the concept of "householder" for "head of household."

Whatever words you use to describe it, a growing percentage of families are maintained by women. In 1985, 19% of all families with one or more children under 18 fell into this category.

This trend is even more pronounced among young families. More than half of all families with young children headed by a person under age 35 were maintained by women in 1985.

Look at it from a child's point of view. In 1985, one out of four children lived with only one parent. And 90% of these lived with their mother.

SEE ALSO 4.16

In 1984, 8.7 million women were living with children under age 21 whose fathers were not living with them.

▲▲▲ Only 46% of these women had been awarded child-support payments from the fathers the previous year.

▲▲▲ Only half of those due child-support payments received the full amount.

▲▲▲ Child-support payments have not kept pace with inflation. In 1983 the average payment (adjusted for inflation) was 15% below the level reported in 1978.

Recent changes in federal law have made it easier to enforce child-support responsibilities. It's too soon to tell whether they will have a significant impact.

**AFDC Payments as a Percentage
of the Poverty Line**

*(median maximum payments
for a family of four)*

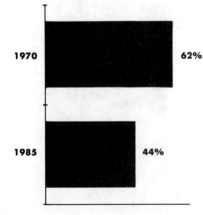

Poor women and children have never received very generous assistance from Aid to Families with Dependent Children. But since 1970, real AFDC benefits have declined.

The fifty states offer widely varying maximum AFDC payments, ranging in 1985, from $675 per month in New York to $147 in Alabama. The benefit level in the middle of this range—the median maximum payment—is a good measure of the typical assistance.

In 1970 the median maximum AFDC payment amounted to $572, or about 62% of the poverty line for a family of four. By 1985 it had declined to $322, or only 44% of the poverty line.

Many poor families were helped by increases in noncash benefits such as food stamps in the 1970s. But in the 1980s, average benefits available through these programs also declined.

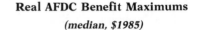

Real AFDC Benefit Maximums

(median, $1985)

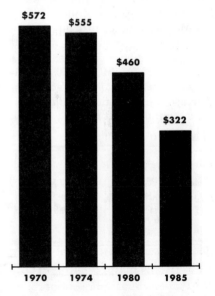

SEE ALSO 7.5, 7.6

Women today enjoy more economic autonomy, but they often pay a high price for it. Women's relative income is determined not only by their earnings but also by the kinds of households they live in.

Married couples normally pool income, while single and divorced women seldom receive a share of a man's income. In the wake of divorce, men's incomes tend to increase, while women's plummet.

Assuming that married women enjoy the same standard of living as their husbands, women's average income can be estimated by weighting their average income in different types of households by the percentage of women in those households. If the percentage of women living in low-income households goes up, all else being equal, women's overall access to income goes down.

By this measure, women's overall access to income relative to men's dropped from 92% in 1967 to 87% in 1985.

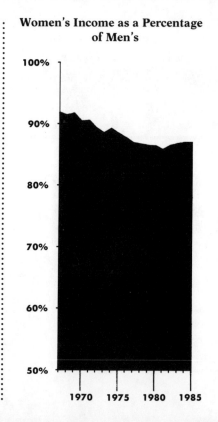

Women's Income as a Percentage of Men's

3.14 □ POOR FAMILIES MAINTAINED BY WOMEN

▲▲

*F*amilies maintained by women have always been particularly vulnerable to poverty, but over the past twenty-five years their situation has worsened. They represented 48% of families with incomes below the poverty level in 1985, a sharp increase from 20% in 1959.

The risk of poverty is particularly high for black and Hispanic families headed by women. More than 50% of these families had incomes below the poverty level in 1985.

This feminization of poverty reflects, in part, the pauperization of motherhood. The more young children a mother has, the more likely she is to live in poverty.

Percentage of All Poor Families Maintained by Women

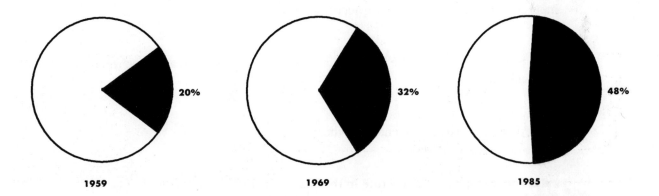

1959   1969   1985

20%   32%   48%

SEE ALSO 3.10, 7.5, 7.6

3.15 □ CONTRACEPTIVE CHOICES?

▲ ▲

Women aren't always able to make their own decisions about childbearing.

▲▲▲ Although the Supreme Court legalized abortion in 1972, married women interviewed in 1982 felt that 27% of their children had been "mistimed" and 8% had been unwanted at the time of conception.

▲▲▲ Many women, women of color in particular, have had sterilization forced on them or performed without full explanation of the consequences. Many others have chosen sterilization as a means of birth control only because no alternative method of safe and reliable contraception was available.

▲▲▲ Since 1980, worldwide funding for reproductive and contraceptive research has declined.

In the U.S., it's probably teenagers who suffer most:

▲▲▲ The teenage pregnancy rate in the U.S. is the highest in the developed world, twice as great as Canada's and seven times that of the Netherlands.

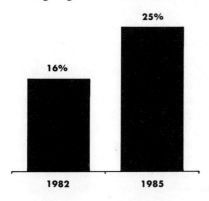

**Percentage of Working Women with a Child
under 5 Using Organized Child-Care Facilities**

Good child care is hard to find. As more women with young children have entered the labor force, parents have increasingly begun to rely on organized child-care facilities. In 1985, 25% of all working women with children under age 5 relied on such facilities, compared to 16% in 1982.

In many areas the demand for child care is much greater than the supply, and waiting lists are long. Furthermore, parents don't always know what kind of care their children are getting. No federal regulations govern child-care centers. And many parents, especially single mothers, can't afford day care. Federal support for it has never been extensive, but since 1981 the funding has been significantly reduced.

Day care isn't the only problem. As of early 1986, only four states—California, Montana, Connecticut, and Massachusetts—had laws specifically protecting the jobs of women who have babies. Less than 40% of working women could expect even six weeks of paid maternity leave. Unlike the U.S., every country in Western Europe guarantees at least fourteen weeks maternity leave, and most provide for more.

▲ ▲

"*D*emocracy," emphasizes the Reverend Jesse Jackson, "doesn't guarantee success—it guarantees opportunity." But what kinds of economic opportunities do people of color have in this country? They are more likely to be poor, more likely to be unemployed, and more likely to die in infancy than white people. The charts in this chapter show that people of color have made important economic gains since the U.S. outlawed racial and ethnic discrimina-

tion more than twenty years ago. The charts also show that many of these gains were partially reversed in the early 1980s.

The chapter begins with an overview of racial and ethnic differences within the U.S. population. Chart 4.1 provides a breakdown of the population by race and ethnic origin in 1985. Chart 4.2 describes recent legal and illegal immigration to the U.S. The geographical distribution of people of color is quite uneven. As Chart 4.3 shows, a very large percentage of blacks live in central cities. Few government statistics exist for American Indians, but Chart 4.4 consolidates some important information about this group.

Wherever people of color live and whatever their origin, they don't have much money to spend. Black, Hispanic, and white families all saw their incomes decline after about 1979, with only a small rebound after 1983, pictured in Chart 4.5. But black and Hispanic families, with far lower incomes to begin with, were much more vulnerable to those declines. The percentage of blacks and Hispanics in poverty increased between 1974 and 1985. As Chart 4.6 shows, almost a third of black people and more than a quarter of Hispanics had incomes below the poverty line in 1985.

Low incomes are partly due to the lack of jobs. When the overall unemployment rate increased in the early

1980s, it increased even more for black and Hispanic workers. As Chart 4.7 shows, the unemployment rate for blacks runs about twice that of whites, with the rate for Hispanics in between. These differences can't be explained away by differences in educational attainment. As Chart 4.8 shows, black college graduates were more likely to be unemployed in 1986 than white high-school graduates.

Blacks and Hispanics are more likely than whites to work in dead-end jobs. Chart 4.9 shows that they are overrepresented in less-skilled service occupations and underrepresented in managerial and professional jobs. In general, the public sector has offered blacks better opportunities than the private sector. As Chart 4.10 shows, black women are particularly likely to work for the government. But as a result, many black families have been hurt by recent cutbacks in government employment.

The most dramatic reversal of historic gains has been the recent decline in the relative wages of people of color. Chart 4.11 shows that blacks, Asians, and Native Americans working full time significantly improved their earnings relative to whites between 1956 and 1976. But between 1979 and 1986, blacks and Hispanics lost ground. Chart 4.12 shows that this was particularly the case for black women between 1977 and 1983.

The affirmative action programs of the 1970s had a small but positive impact on job opportunities for people of color, but these efforts, summarized in Chart 4.13, have been cut back. As Chart 4.14 shows, significant inequalities remain in access to education. Yet in recent years financial aid to college students has declined.

People of color have a lot of children to take care of. Many of these children live in families maintained by women (see Charts 4.15 and 4.16). Many of these children grow up in poverty, in homes that lack many of the amenities described in Chart 4.17, such as a telephone or car. And infant-mortality statistics for black children suggest that many are denied the most basic opportunity of all. Chart 4.18 shows that they are twice as likely as their white counterparts to die before reaching their first birthday.

4.1 □ RACIAL AND ETHNIC COMPOSITION OF THE U.S.

The U.S. has traditionally been described as a melting pot for peoples of very diverse backgrounds and histories. But in 1980 about a fifth of the U.S. population had racial or ethnic backgrounds that set them apart from the culturally and politically dominant white population.

Blacks and Hispanics accounted for 12% and 7% respectively, of the U.S. population. Asians and Pacific Islanders made up 1.6% and American Indians, Eskimos, and Aleuts 0.6%. Because these groups are concentrated in certain geographic areas, they often represent a much larger percentage of the population in their own communities.

About 61% of Hispanics trace their family origins to Mexico, while about 15% are from Puerto Rican backgrounds.

All of these groups are growing faster than the white population.

Racial and Ethnic Composition of U.S. Population, 1985

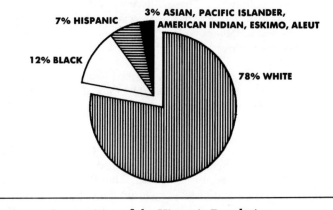

Composition of the Hispanic Population

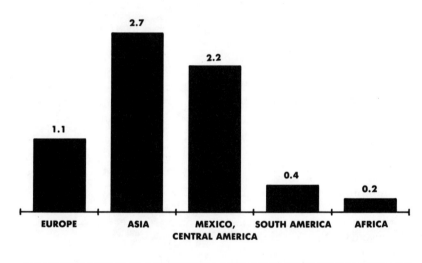

Legal Immigrants to the U.S., 1971–84 *(millions)*

2.7				
2.2				
1.1		0.4	0.2	

EUROPE   ASIA   MEXICO, CENTRAL AMERICA   SOUTH AMERICA   AFRICA

Illegal immigrants living in the U.S. in 1985: Estimated between 3 million and 6 million, or between about 1.2% and 2.5% of the U.S. population.

The Statue of Liberty doesn't see nearly as many immigrants as she used to. But immigration to the U.S. is still substantial. About 6.5 million people legally immigrated between 1971 and 1984. Estimates of the size of the illegal-resident population range from about 3 million to 6 million. Overall, immigration accounts for about 40% of our population growth every year.

Asians predominate among legal immigrants, largely because the U.S. granted political-refugee status to many individuals fleeing Vietnam, Laos, and Cambodia. Many Cubans were also admitted for the same reason. The U.S. is far less willing to admit refugees from countries that are our official allies, such as El Salvador.

Most illegal immigrants come from Mexico and Central America, where economic conditions have worsened in recent years.

4.3 □ IN THE CITY OR IN THE COUNTRY?

Percentage of the Population Living in Central Cities in 1980

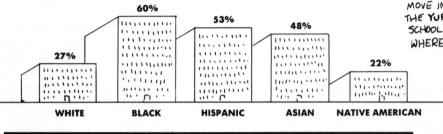

WHITE	BLACK	HISPANIC	ASIAN	NATIVE AMERICAN
27%	60%	53%	48%	22%

CHECK IT OUT. THE REASON **WE** LIVE IN THE CITY IS TO KEEP THE RENTS DOWN SO THE ARTISTS CAN MOVE IN AND FRESH UP THE NEIGHBORHOOD SO THE **YUPPIES** CAN MIGRATE FROM GRADUATE SCHOOL AND PUSH **US** OUT TO THE SUBURBS WHERE THEY JUST **DYING** TO HAVE US.

Most people of color live in central cities. As a result, they are especially vulnerable to central-city problems such as inadequate housing, high crime rates, and poor schools.

High urban concentration, combined with geographic distribution, sometimes makes minorities into majorities. By 1982, blacks made up more than 50% of the population of such major cities as Washington, D.C., Richmond, and Newark. Hispanics accounted for more than 35% of the population of Albuquerque and San Antonio, while blacks and Hispanics together constituted a majority or close to it in Los Angeles, Chicago, and the New York borough of Brooklyn.

Native Americans (American Indians, Eskimos, and Aleuts) are more likely than whites to live in the country. In 1980, only about 22% lived in central cities.

4.4 ☐ AMERICAN INDIANS

▲▲▲ In 1980, American Indians accounted for slightly less than 1% of the population and were concentrated in four states: California, Oklahoma, Arizona, and New Mexico.

▲▲▲ Only about 25% of Indians, primarily the young and the elderly, lived on reservations; most Indians of working age were forced to seek jobs elsewhere.

▲▲▲ In 1980, about 27% of American Indian households had incomes under the poverty line—some of them were the poorest of the poor.

▲▲▲ Since the Reagan administration came into office, federal spending for Indian and Alaska Native programs has been reduced by about a third.

SEE ALSO T.6

*M*ost black and Hispanic families must get by on far less income than white families. And despite some improvements in the mid-1980s, their inflation-adjusted incomes were still lower in 1985 than they had been in 1972.

A continuing increase in the proportion of families maintained by women pulled median income down. Families with both husband and wife present fared better.

The Cosby Show notwithstanding, few families of color enjoy an upper-middle-class standard of living. While 20% of white families received more than $50,000 in 1985, only 7% of black families and only 8% of Hispanic families made that much.

Blacks and Hispanics are also far less likely to enjoy income from ownership rather than work. Less than 1% received more than $10,000 in property income in 1983.

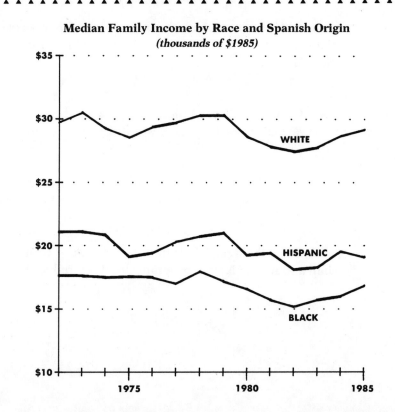

Median Family Income by Race and Spanish Origin
(thousands of $1985)

SEE ALSO 7.1

*T*t's nothing new. Discrimination and unemployment have long left blacks and Hispanics more susceptible to poverty than whites.

For a while, things were getting better. Between 1959 and 1974, government anti-poverty programs, along with relatively low unemployment rates, lowered the overall poverty rate and reduced the differences in poverty rates between blacks and whites.

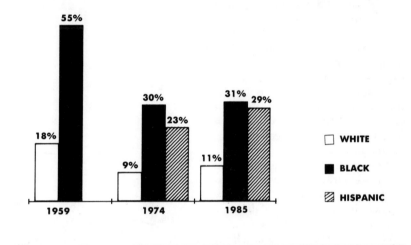

Percent of Persons Below Poverty Level by Race and Spanish Origin

□ WHITE

■ BLACK

▨ HISPANIC

But after 1974, all those trends were reversed. Cuts in federal social spending had a very uneven impact. In 1981 alone, the average black family lost three times as much in benefits as the average white family, and the average Hispanic family lost twice as much.

SEE ALSO 7.3, 7.4

4.7 ☐ LAST HIRED

▲▲

*H*igh unemployment rates afflict blacks and Hispanics more than whites. In 1986, 14.8% of black workers and 10.6% of Hispanic workers couldn't find jobs, while 6.8% of whites were in the same predicament.

Teenagers had an even harder time. In the last quarter of 1986, 36% of black, 20% of Hispanic, and 15% of white workers between the ages of 16 and 19 were unemployed.

Persistently high unemployment rates discourage people from looknig for work. Black male labor-force participation rates have dropped considerably in recent years.

When people of color bear a large share of the burden of unemployment, they buffer whites against the ups and downs of the business cycle.

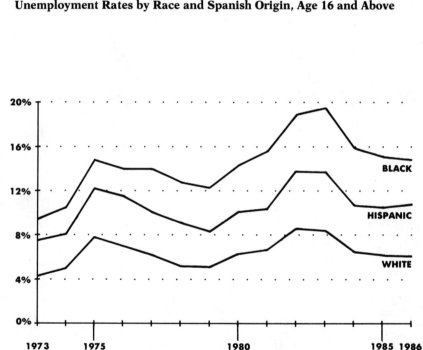

Unemployment Rates by Race and Spanish Origin, Age 16 and Above

SEE ALSO 2.9, 2.11

▲▲

Youth Unemployment by Educational Attainment in 1986 *(ages 16–24)*

	LESS THAN 4 YRS. HIGH SCHOOL	HIGH SCHOOL (4 YRS.)	COLLEGE (4 YRS. OR MORE)
WHITE	20.3%	10.1%	5.3%
BLACK	44.0%	26.6%	13.2%
HISPANIC	20.3%	14.6%	4.6%

A college education always helps. But a diploma doesn't guarantee protection against unemployment or discrimination. Even with a college degree, blacks and Hispanics had higher unemployment rates than their white counterparts in 1986.

SEE ALSO 2.9, 2.11

4.9 ☐ MORE MENIAL WORK

▲▲▲

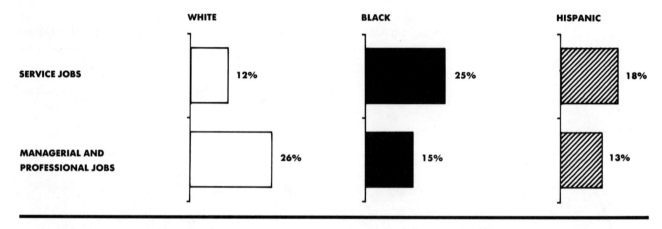

Occupational Comparisons, 1985

WHITE • BLACK • HISPANIC

SERVICE JOBS — 12% / 25% / 18%

MANAGERIAL AND PROFESSIONAL JOBS — 26% / 15% / 13%

Discrimination has historically limited people of color to jobs whites wanted to avoid, such as housecleaning. Today, they remain disproportionately represented in jobs that involve housecleaning for the economy as a whole, such as cleaning buildings, preparing food, waiting on tables, and caring for children.

About a quarter of all blacks and almost a fifth of all Hispanics are employed at the low end of the occupational ladder, in low-paying service jobs.

In managerial and professional specialty occupations, people of color are underrepresented. More than a quarter of all white workers hold such jobs, compared to only 15% of black workers and 13% of Hispanic workers.

4.10 □ MORE LIKELY TO WORK FOR THE GOVERNMENT

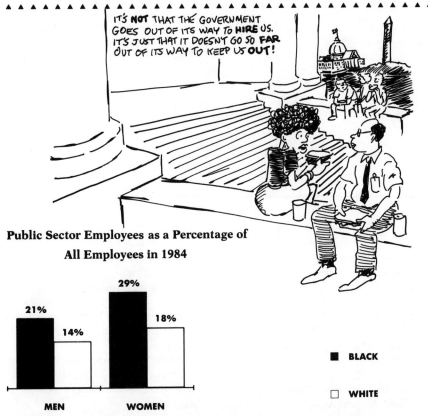

Public Sector Employees as a Percentage of All Employees in 1984

21% · 14% · MEN

29% · 18% · WOMEN

■ BLACK

□ WHITE

In recent years blacks have found more jobs in the public sector than in the private. After 1950, the percentage of black workers in government jobs grew rapidly, peaking in the mid-1970s. In 1984, about 29% of all employed black women and 21% of black men worked for federal, state, or local governments. The corresponding percentages for whites were far lower.

Blacks employed in the public sector tend to earn more relative to whites than their black counterparts in the private sector, perhaps because antidiscrimination policies and affirmative-action efforts have had less impact on the private sector.

Under the Reagan administration, however, public-sector jobs have decreased due to budget cuts. These cutbacks help explain increased black unemployment.

SEE ALSO 6.2

4.11 □ WAGE INEQUALITIES

▲▲▲

Median Annual Earnings of Blacks, Asians, and Native Americans as a Percentage of White Earnings
(full-time workers)

	1956	1970	1976
WOMEN	56%	85%	94%
MEN	62%	70%	75%

Median Weekly Earnings of Blacks and Hispanics Relative to Whites
(full-time workers)

	1979	1986
BLACK WOMEN	93%	90%
BLACK MEN	76%	73%
HISPANIC WOMEN	83%	82%
HISPANIC MEN	74%	69%

DON'T YOU GET THE FEELING THAT THE FIFTIES ARE ON THEIR WAY BACK?

WHITE GO-GO BOOTS, THE HONEYMOONERS, HAIR CREAM, FORMICA, PINK AND TURQUOISE... DONTCHA JUST LOVE IT?

I WAS THINKING MORE ABOUT THE LOW WAGES.

*B*etween 1956 and 1976, blacks, Asians, and Native American workers (all labeled "nonwhite" by the Census Bureau) narrowed the gap between their earnings and those of white workers. After 1979, however, data for blacks and Hispanic workers suggest that the gap began to widen.

By 1976, full-time women workers from these diverse backgrounds enjoyed median annual earnings about 94% those of white women.

Their male counterparts were limited to smaller gains—and to 75% of the earnings of white men.

Government agencies discontinued collecting economic data for blacks, Asians, and Native Americans as a group in 1978, and began collecting separate data for blacks and Hispanics.

Both blacks and Hispanics saw their earnings decline slightly relative to those of whites between 1979 and 1986.

SEE ALSO 2.6

*B*lacks, like most other people of color, suffer a double disadvantage in the labor market. They are less likely to find a job, and when they do, it pays less. One way to measure the combined effect is to multiply the median earnings of the different groups by the percentage of the labor force of that group that is employed. This provides an estimate of the typical earnings of a member of the labor force.

The typical labor-force earnings of blacks relative to whites—the black labor-force earnings ratio—is far lower than the ratio of relative earnings for employed workers. Individual black men working full time in 1983 earned about 75% of what white men earned, but a typical black man in the labor force earned only 52% of what a typical white man earned—because the black man was far more likely to be unemployed.

The trends in black labor-force earnings ratios confirm that relative black gains were reversed in the late 1970s and early 1980s. These ratios have declined for both black men and women since 1977.

Median Earnings of a Typical Member of the Black Labor Force Relative to a Typical Member of the White Labor Force

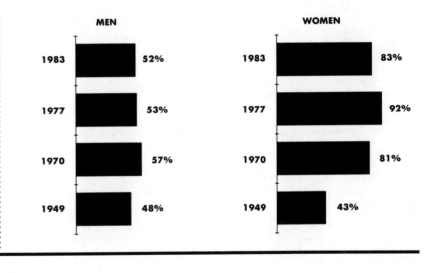

MEN

1983	52%
1977	53%
1970	57%
1949	48%

WOMEN

1983	83%
1977	92%
1970	81%
1949	43%

▲▲▲ Several studies have shown that federal affirmative action programs had a small but significant impact on racial discrimination. The Labor Department recently found that federal contractors required to comply with affirmative-action guidelines increased their minority employment rates by 20% between 1974 and 1980, while contractors not subject to the guidelines raised their minority participation rates by just 12% during the same period.

▲▲▲ The Reagan administration has publicly opposed any affirmative-action programs that use goals and timetables to assure compliance. It has also significantly cut back efforts to enforce the Civil Rights Act:

—from 1981 to 1983, total real federal outlays on civil rights and equal employment opportunity declined by 9%.

—the budget of the Office of Federal Contract Compliance was cut by 24%.

—between 1981 and 1984 the number of cases of labor discrimination brought by the federal government dropped by 24%, even though the number of complaints brought by individuals increased 68%.

4.14 □ THE EDUCATION GAP PERSISTS

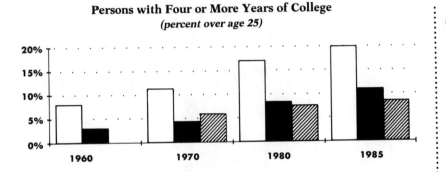

Persons with Four or More Years of College
(percent over age 25)

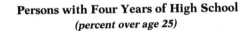

Persons with Four Years of High School
(percent over age 25)

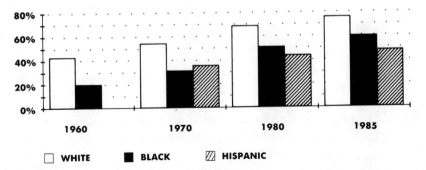

□ WHITE   ■ BLACK   ▨ HISPANIC

"Campus populations are turning noticeably paler," noted a recent *Wall Street Journal* article. Racial and ethnic differences in education have always been greatest on the college level, and few gains were made between 1980 and 1985.

Since 1950, blacks have made significant progress in getting high-school diplomas, but in 1985 less than 60% of blacks and Hispanics over age 25 had completed four or more years of high school. Many of the high schools they attended were highly segregated.

Cuts in aid for college students reinforced a decline in the percentage of black and Hispanic high-school graduates going on to college. Budget cuts also shrank tutorial and counseling programs for disadvantaged students.

SEE ALSO 7.13

4.15 □ WHO'S BRINGING UP THE KIDS?

*B*lack and Hispanic families have more kids. In 1985, fewer than half of all white families had any children under age 18, compared to 59% of black and 66% of Hispanic families. And less

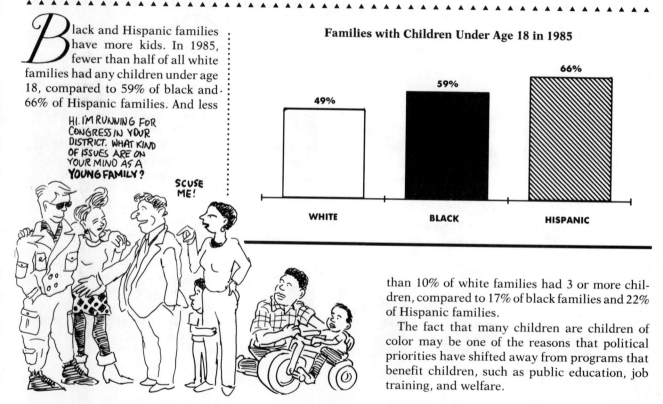

Families with Children Under Age 18 in 1985

WHITE	BLACK	HISPANIC
49%	59%	66%

HI. I'M RUNNING FOR CONGRESS IN YOUR DISTRICT. WHAT KIND OF ISSUES ARE ON YOUR MIND AS A **YOUNG FAMILY?**

SCUSE ME!

than 10% of white families had 3 or more children, compared to 17% of black families and 22% of Hispanic families.

The fact that many children are children of color may be one of the reasons that political priorities have shifted away from programs that benefit children, such as public education, job training, and welfare.

SEE ALSO 7.5

4.16 ☐ MANY BLACK AND HISPANIC WOMEN MAINTAIN FAMILIES

▲▲

Families Maintained by Women
(as a percent of all families)

1960   **1985**

BLACK  22%

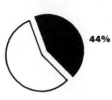 44%

WHITE  9%

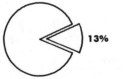 13%

HISPANIC 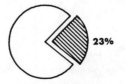 23%

*B*lack and Hispanic families are even more likely to be maintained by women alone than white families. In 1985, 44% of all black families fell into this category, as opposed to 23% of Hispanic families and 13% of white families.

Some social scientists argue that public-assistance programs lead to more families without adult men. But the programs vary considerably across states, and the percentage of families maintained by women is not significantly lower in states with low benefits. High unemployment rates among black and Hispanic men are probably a more important factor.

SEE ALSO 3.10, 3.14

4.17 ☐ FEWER HOUSES AND FEWER CARS

1980	WHITE	BLACK	HISPANIC	AMERICAN INDIAN, ESKIMO, ALEUT	ASIAN OR PACIFIC ISLANDER
OWNER-OCCUPIED HOUSING	68%	44%	53%	53%	43%
INCOMPLETE PLUMBING	2%	6%	11%	3%	4%
NO PHONE	6%	16%	28%	5%	17%
NO VEHICLE	10%	33%	18%	16%	22%

4.18 ☐ DEATH AT AN EARLIER AGE

▲▲

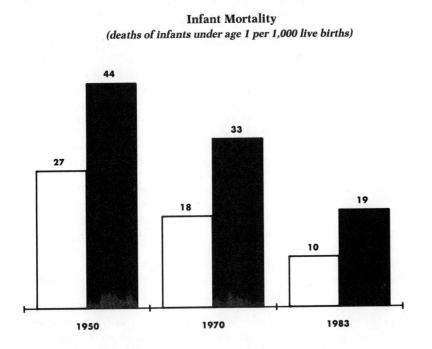

Infant Mortality
(deaths of infants under age 1 per 1,000 live births)

☐ WHITE ■ BLACK

*B*lack infants have a greater chance of survival than they once did. But they still face twice the risk of death that white infants face.

During 1982 and 1983, the mortality rate for white infants dropped by 8.1%, while for black infants it rose by 1.5%. This increase was the first reversal in a consistent fall in black infant mortality rates since 1960.

The U.S. health-care system is not very good at providing prenatal care or medical assistance for low-income mothers. Fourteen other countries have infant mortality rates lower than ours.

▲▲▲

"*What's* the difference between a farmer and a pigeon?" begins a common joke in farm country. The answer: a pigeon can still make a deposit on a tractor. U.S. farmers are in serious economic trouble. They can produce more food more efficiently than ever before, but they have a hard time selling what they produce at a price that allows them to break even, much less turn a profit.

As Chart 5.1 shows, farmers have been leaving the farm for a long time. Technological change in agriculture has reduced the need for labor and made it difficult for small farms to compete. Net farm income, pictured in Chart 5.2, has declined at a particularly sharp rate since the mid-1970s.

Middlemen such as food processors, packagers, and marketers often wield enough market power to protect their profit margins, while farmers bear the burden of fluctuating prices. Chart 5.3 documents the decline in the share of the consumer's food dollar that goes to the farmer. Chart 5.4 provides another insight into farmers' economic problems. Prices farmers paid for equipment and supplies have increased steadily in the 1980s, while prices they received for farm products have stagnated.

Despite these problems, farmers in the 1970s benefited from a boom in agricultural real estate that increased the value of their most important asset, land. Convinced that the key to successful farming lay in new equipment, farmers borrowed heavily in order to invest. Then agricultural prices and land values fell. Charts 5.5 and 5.6 detail the increase in farm indebtedness.

Things wouldn't have been so bad for U.S. farmers if they had been able to increase their sales to consumers in other countries. Farm exports had grown dramatically in the late 1970s. Unfortunately, as Chart 5.7 shows, they leveled off in the early 1980s. The high value of the dollar made U.S. grain expensive overseas, and record levels of world grain production in 1985 and 1986 glutted international markets. Even the small declines in world production shares pictured in Chart 5.8 signaled problems for U.S. farmers.

In late 1985, these economic difficulties helped persuade Congress to renew its commitment to farm-price supports. As Chart 5.9 shows, the cost of these supports has increased. And many critics feel that they don't address the underlying problems of U.S. agriculture. In the long run, the U.S. will have to confront the basic agricultural dilemma: some people grow more food than they can sell, while others need more food than they can buy. Chart 5.10 illustrates the unhappy fact that more food doesn't always mean less hunger.

Farmers are not the only ones who have suffered from problems in farm country. As Chart 5.11 shows, farm laborers are among the lowest paid workers in the country. And sooner or later attention will have to return to the land itself, where the intensive use of chemicals, pictured in Chart 5.12, threatens the future of the rural environment.

5.1 □ FEWER FARMERS

▲▲▲▲ ▲▲▲▲ ▲▲▲▲ ▲▲▲▲ ▲▲▲▲ ▲▲▲▲ ▲▲▲▲ ▲▲▲▲ ▲▲▲▲ ▲▲▲▲ ▲▲▲▲ ▲▲▲▲ ▲▲▲▲ ▲▲▲

Old McDonald had a farm, but now he may be flipping hamburgers! It's been happening for a long time. Between 1950 and 1985, the proportion of the U.S. population living on farms dropped from about 15% to less than 4%. Yet farms produce more now than ever before, because of increases in the productivity of land and labor.

Technological change has transformed U.S. agriculture. Farming now utilizes more machinery per unit output than industry. Between 1950 and 1985, the average size of farms more than doubled.

The growth of "factories in the field" has provided some benefits to consumers, but it has also threatened farming as a way of life.

Farm Population as a Percentage of Total U.S. Population

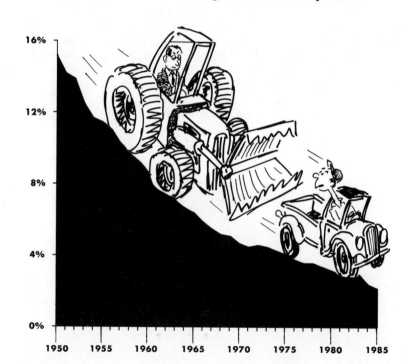

SEE ALSO 2.2

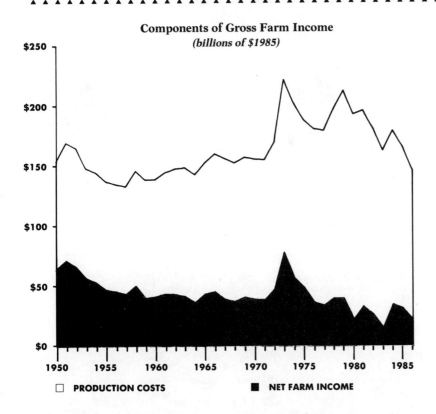

Components of Gross Farm Income
(billions of $1985)

□ PRODUCTION COSTS　　　■ NET FARM INCOME

A modern farm costs a lot of money to run, but it doesn't pay very much.

What farmers earn is called net farm income, the difference between the value of their product and their costs of production. In 1950, net farm income amounted to about 43% of production costs, a pretty good return on investment. By the early 1980s, however, it averaged about 11%. Real net farm income was lower in 1986 than it was in 1950.

Small farms have been hurt the most. On average, those with sales under $20,000 didn't receive any net farm income between 1980 and 1984—they suffered major losses. In 1984, large farms with sales of more than $500,000—about 1% of all farms—took in 50% of all net farm income.

Many rural people are poor. In 1983, 24% of the farm population lived under the poverty line, compared to 15% of the nonfarm population.

5.3 □ A SMALLER SHARE OF THE FOOD DOLLAR

▲▲

*F*armers get only a small share of what you spend at the grocery store, and even that share is decreasing. In 1984, twenty-seven cents out of every food dollar went to the farm, down from thirty-three cents in 1960.

Increases in the amount of money spent on marketing and sales account for much of this change. In 1983, while farm prices fell, food prices actually rose by almost 2%.

The retail food industry is dominated by large firms that are growing larger. In 1985, for instance, the R. J. Reynolds company purchased Nabisco for almost $5 billion. Now Oreo cookies, Ritz crackers, Salem and Camel cigarettes, Planter's nuts, Baby Ruth candy, Del Monte foods, and Kentucky Fried Chicken are all made by the same company.

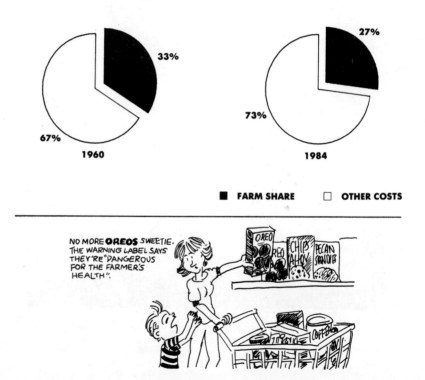

The Farm Share of Consumer Food Costs

33%

67%

1960

27%

73%

1984

■ FARM SHARE   □ OTHER COSTS

NO MORE **OREOS** SWEETIE. THE WARNING LABEL SAYS THEY'RE "DANGEROUS FOR THE FARMER'S HEALTH".

5.4 ☐ THE UPS AND DOWNS OF AGRICULTURAL PRICES

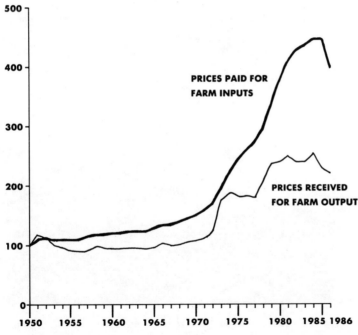

Indices of Prices Paid and Prices Received by Farmers
(1950 = 100)

PRICES PAID FOR FARM INPUTS

PRICES RECEIVED FOR FARM OUTPUT

*T*armers have had a hard time with prices. Throughout most of the postwar period, the prices of industrial goods, including most farm equipment and supplies, rose fairly steadily. Prices of farm products, such as wheat, fluctuated more and increased less.

Part of the explanation lies in the long time it takes to grow crops or raise animals. Prices may be high when a farmer plants his field or breeds his stock, but low by the time he is ready to sell what he has produced. That makes it hard for a farmer to plan or adjust.

Two other factors are important. Agriculture is more competitive than most other industries. And family farms can't hedge their bets with other investments. If farm prices go down, they have to produce more to stay even. Unfortunately, increased production leads to still lower prices.

*T*n 1950, farmers owed about ten cents for every dollar of assets. By 1986, they owed more than twenty-four cents on that dollar.

Throughout the 1970s, debt continued to grow, but the value of farm assets grew just as fast, so debts as a percentage of assets remained fairly constant. In fact, bankers encouraged farmers to borrow more money because of rapid increases in the value of agricultural land. Between 1977 and 1981, real estate speculation increased values by 30% or more in some states, such as Nebraska.

In the 1980s, a number of factors completely outside the control of farmers hurt their sales, and some land values fell by more than 20%. Suddenly, farmer's debts loomed large.

Farm Debt as a Percentage of Farm Assets

Family Size Farms in Debt in 1985

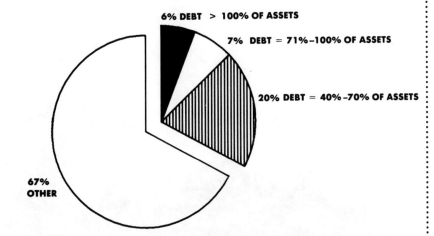

6% DEBT > 100% OF ASSETS

7% DEBT = 71%–100% OF ASSETS

20% DEBT = 40%–70% OF ASSETS

67% OTHER

*T*n 1985, about a third of all family-size commercial farms in the U.S. were dangerously in debt. Things were bad enough for the 20% of these farms that had debts amounting between 40% and 70% of their assets. But bankruptcy was almost inevitable for the 6% whose debts were greater than their assets.

When farmers can't make their payments, banks can't always pay their own debts. In 1985, 61% of all bank failures involved agricultural banks. The Farm Credit System reported a $2.7 billion loss in 1985, the largest annual deficit posted by a U.S. financial institution.

Trouble for farmers can mean trouble for the economy as a whole.

▲ ▲

*F*arm goods are one of our country's leading exports. In the early 1980s, almost one dollar in every four that farmers received came from abroad.

But a lot of things can come between a farmer and that export dollar. Foreign consumers can't afford U.S. agricultural products when the current exchange rate makes their prices too expensive. The high dollar of the early 1980s put a big dent in overseas sales.

Also, U.S. farmers face increased competition from abroad, from developing countries as well as from the European Economic Community. Although the value of the dollar declined in 1985, the U.S. experienced its first trade deficit in agricultural goods in at least two decades.

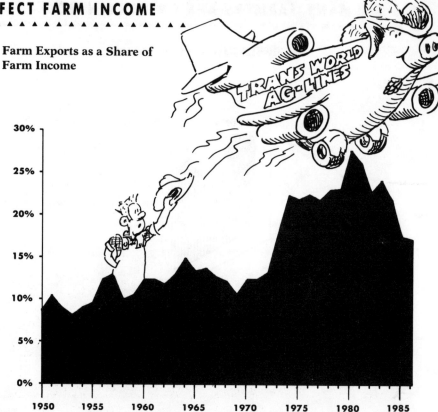

Farm Exports as a Share of Farm Income

SEE ALSO 10.5, 10.8

5.8 □ A SMALLER SHARE OF WORLD MARKETS

▲▲

The U.S. is still the breadbasket for much of the world. In 1986, U.S. farmers produced 60% of the world's soybeans, 43% of the world's corn, and 12% of the world's wheat. But the U.S. share of wheat and soybean production declined between 1976 and 1986, and further declines were expected in 1987.

Despite widespread hunger in many countries, the world market was glutted with grain in 1985 and 1986. Improved production practices have allowed many countries that normally import food to export it. In April 1986, a record 200 million metric tons of grain were stored around the world.

Protectionist policies abroad have also limited U.S. farm exports. The European Economic Community restricts sales of American wheat and soybeans.

U.S. Share of Total World Production of Grains

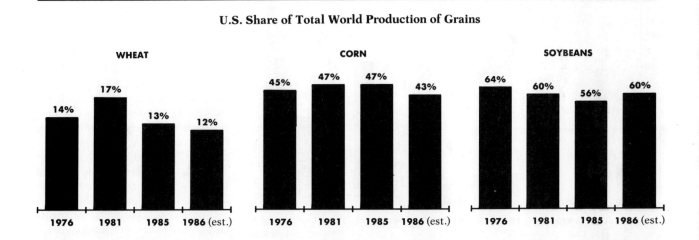

WHEAT

1976: 14%
1981: 17%
1985: 13%
1986 (est.): 12%

CORN

1976: 45%
1981: 47%
1985: 47%
1986 (est.): 43%

SOYBEANS

1976: 64%
1981: 60%
1985: 56%
1986 (est.): 60%

▲ ▲

Commodity Credit Corporation Costs *(billions of $1985)*

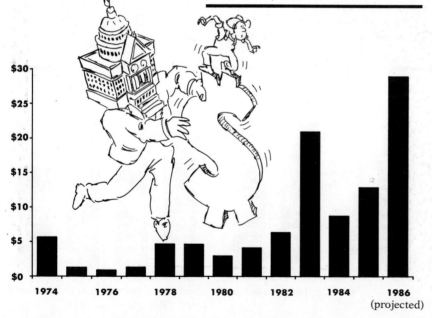

G overnment price-support policies can make or break farmers. Almost all developed countries provide some government protection from the ups and downs of agricultural prices. The U.S. government first began supporting farm prices during the Great Depression of the 1930s. At that time, the program cost less than a penny for every dollar of farm profits.

In the early 1980s, the cost of supporting prices went through the roof. In 1985 the Commodity Credit Corporation, which is charged with the task, spent about forty-three cents for every dollar of profit farmers made.

Congress approved legislation in 1985 that lowered farm-price supports and set aggressive goals for increasing farm exports. The new policy is not likely to diminish the overall cost of the supports.

Nor is it likely to help those farmers with the biggest debts. Because federal payments are based on how much a farmer grows, only about seventeen cents per dollar of profits will go to full-time farmers in desperate straits.

▲ ▲

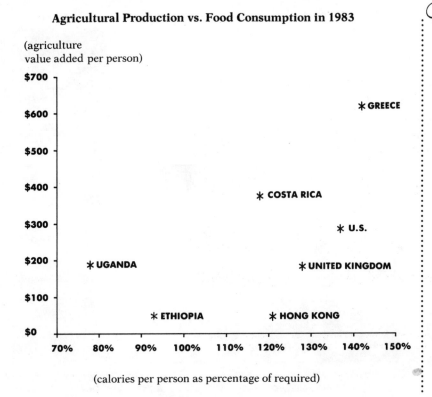

Agricultural Production vs. Food Consumption in 1983

(agriculture value added per person)

(calories per person as percentage of required)

*W*hile the U.S. and most European countries pay farmers not to over-produce, many people worldwide go hungry. Ethiopia and Uganda are only the extreme examples.

You might think that the productivity of a country's agriculture determines how well its citizens eat. But it's not so simple. Uganda produces the same value of agricultural goods per person as Great Britain but exports most of it as coffee.

Industrialization can help. Both famine-ridden Ethiopia and densely populated Hong Kong produce very few farm goods per person. But while many Ethiopians go hungry, Hong Kong can pay for imported food with money from exports of manufactured exports.

In the long run, economic growth could solve the problem of global hunger—but only if the fruits of growth are served up to those who need them the most.

5.11 □ FARMWORKERS GET LOW WAGES

▲▲

*W*age earners who work on farms have a hard time making a living. Most agricultural work is seasonal and low-paying. About 69% of all farmhands in 1985 worked less than 150 days and earned only $934. Even workers who worked almost full time earned on average only $8,322.

In addition, farmwork is dangerous. In 1979, only miners and construction workers had higher on-the-job death rates than those working on U.S. farms. Migrant farmworkers are particularly vulnerable to health problems caused by lack of sanitation facilities and exposure to pesticides.

Although official statistics show a sharp decline in the population of migrant farm laborers in recent years, such statistics don't include illegal immigrants. By all accounts, their numbers are increasing.

Farmworkers and Their Annual Wages in 1985
($1985)

$8,322

$934

**WORKED LESS THAN 150 DAYS A YEAR
(69% OF ALL FARMWORKERS)**

**WORKED MORE THAN 150 DAYS
A YEAR (31% OF ALL FARMWORKERS)**

▲▲

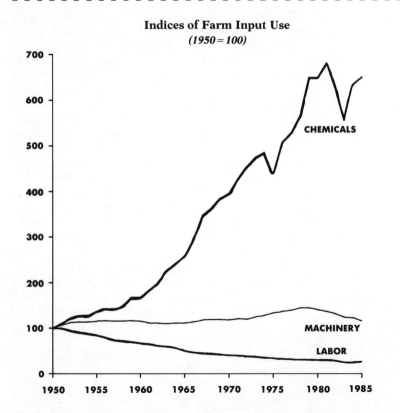

Indices of Farm Input Use
(1950 = 100)

As the farm becomes more of a factory in the field, it also becomes more of an environmental hazard. In 1977, U.S. farms used more than twice as much pesticide, and about one and a half times as much fertilizer, as in 1967. Since the late 1970s the growth rate of pesticide and fertilizer use has slowed but mostly because many farmers cut back on production.

Some pesticides, such as DDT, have been restricted because they pose a major threat to wildlife and to humans. The health effects of many other pesticides remain unclear. Agricultural fertilizer has been identified as a major cause of water pollution. And particularly in the southwest, irrigation has placed heavy demands on limited supplies of groundwater.

▲▲

"*L*ess government is better government," declared President Reagan in his first inaugural speech. Reagan administration policies put government spending and taxation in the political spotlight, but there is little evidence that the policies either reduced or improved the government's role in the economy. Two big changes are apparent: military spending has increased and government deficits have reached unprecedented levels.

Chart 6.1 provides an overview of government spending, which continued on its historic upward trend between 1980 and 1986. Despite this increase, government employment declined as a percentage of the labor force, particularly on the state and local levels, as Chart 6.2 shows. Government workers in general have been hurt by recent cutbacks.

How does U.S. government spending compare with other countries competing in the world market? Chart 6.3 suggests that U.S. social spending was fairly low and military spending very high by international standards in 1981. Chart 6.4 provides an overview of the shifting federal budget priorities. By 1986, military spending had increased to almost a third of the total budget. The cost of financing the deficit was apparent in the increased share of net interest payments.

The following charts trace the expenditures in these budget categories since 1962. Chart 6.5 delineates the hefty increases in expenditures on weapons that boosted real military spending almost to the levels of the peak Vietnam War years. Chart 6.6 documents continued increases in funding for Social Security and Medicare.

Social spending, on the other hand, reached a plateau carved out of the budgets for health, education, natural resources, and transportation. These cutbacks are documented in Chart 6.7. Expenditures for "safety net" programs for poor people were reduced per individual, but Chart 6.8 shows a rising trend, because high poverty and unemployment levels increased the number of applicants for public assistance.

As federal revenue became increasingly dependent on taxes on personal income after 1950, the stage was set for tax reform (see Chart 6.9). As Chart 6.10 shows, the 1981 tax reforms accentuated the historic trend toward decreased corporate income taxes. The same reforms increased taxes on the poor and cut taxes for the rich. The overall cut in personal income tax revenues was counterbalanced somewhat by increases in Social Security taxes (see Chart 6.11). Tax reforms implemented in 1986 were designed partly to increase corporate income taxes and lighten the load on poor and low-income families. But as Chart 6.12 shows, the rich will enjoy the greatest absolute savings.

The 1986 tax reforms were intended to be basically "revenue-neutral"—neither to raise nor to lower total tax revenue. If they succeed in that respect, the future of the federal deficit will depend on whether Congress cuts government spending. But chart 6.13 suggests that every time politicians promise to balance the budget, the opposite seems to happen.

Chart 6.14 breaks down the different components of the increase in the government deficit from 1980 to 1986. It lays the blame on increased military spending, decreased taxes, and higher interest payments due to the deficit itself.

▲▲

Some people see government spending as a cancer, threatening the health of the economy as a whole. But it has grown largely in response to problems that the private sector of the economy could not solve.

In 1950, government spending amounted to 23% of the gross national product (GNP), partly as a result of efforts to reduce unemployment rates, which during the Great Depression reached 25%. The increased military spending necessitated by World War II also expanded the federal budget.

Since that time, the same trends have accelerated on the federal level, while state and local governments have increased spending on roads and education. By 1986, total government spending had reached 38% of GNP.

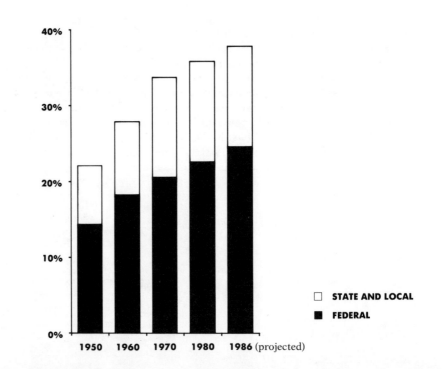

Total Government Spending as a Percentage of GNP

□ STATE AND LOCAL
■ FEDERAL

▲ ▲

*I*nitially, the growth of government spending increased the relative number of government employees. By 1970, about 16% of all civilian workers were employed by the government. After 1970, however, this share dropped, reaching 14% in 1984.

The Reagan administration has been more successful cutting the number of government employees than the amount of government spending. In 1983, there were actually fewer federal employees than in 1970, though state and local governments added about 3 million workers during that time.

Government workers provide a wide variety of services. More than 40% are involved in education, 13% in public health and welfare services, and 8% in police, fire, or sanitation work.

Women and people of color are more likely than other workers to be employed in the public sector, and the differences in pay between men and women, and between whites and people of color, are smaller there than in the private sector.

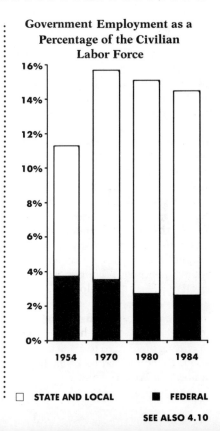

Government Employment as a Percentage of the Civilian Labor Force

□ STATE AND LOCAL   ■ FEDERAL

SEE ALSO 4.10

6.3 ☐ GOVERNMENT SPENDING IN OTHER COUNTRIES

▲▲

*H*ow much do the governments of other major industrial nations spend compared to the U.S.? The share of government spending was lowest in Japan at 35% of the gross domestic product (GDP) in 1981. In the U.S. the share of government (federal, state, and local) was only slightly larger—38%.

In the Western European countries, particularly the social democracies such as Austria and the Scandinavian countries, government spending is much higher. Even in West Germany, a major competitor in foreign trade, government spending accounts for 50% of GDP.

One category of government spending is much higher in the U.S. than elsewhere. In 1981, military spending amounted to 5% of GDP in the U.S., compared to 1% in Japan and 3% in West Germany.

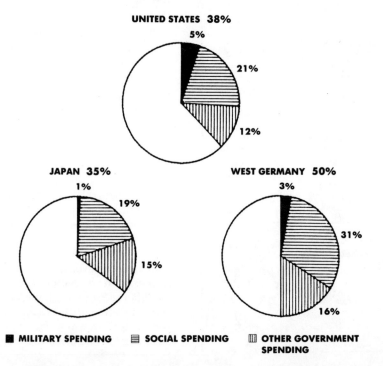

Components of Government Spending as a Percentage of GDP in 1981

UNITED STATES 38%

JAPAN 35%

WEST GERMANY 50%

■ MILITARY SPENDING   ▤ SOCIAL SPENDING   ▥ OTHER GOVERNMENT SPENDING

SEE ALSO 10.2

6.4 □ WHERE FEDERAL DOLLARS GO

Components of the Federal Budget

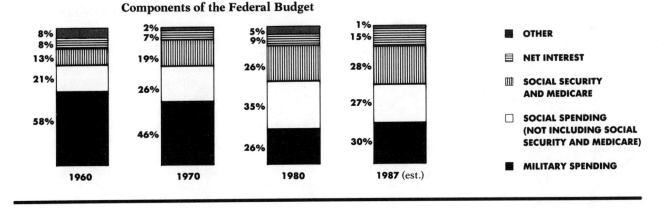

1960
- 8%
- 8%
- 13%
- 21%
- 58%

1970
- 2%
- 7%
- 19%
- 26%
- 46%

1980
- 5%
- 9%
- 26%
- 35%
- 26%

1987 (est.)
- 1%
- 15%
- 28%
- 27%
- 30%

■ OTHER

▤ NET INTEREST

▥ SOCIAL SECURITY AND MEDICARE

□ SOCIAL SPENDING (NOT INCLUDING SOCIAL SECURITY AND MEDICARE)

■ MILITARY SPENDING

Federal dollars are largely divided between military spending, Social Security and Medicare, social programs, and interest on the national debt. The wars in Korea and Vietnam kept military spending at about 50% of the total between 1950 and 1970. By 1980, however, with the U.S. at peace, military spending had dropped to 26%.

As the military's share declined between 1970 and 1980, the share of Social Security and Medicare increased, from 19% to 26%, and the share of social spending increased more sharply, from 26% to 35%.

Between 1980 and 1987, these trends were largely reversed. Military spending grew to 30%, and social spending was cut to 28%. The ballooning federal deficit, financed at very high interest rates, increased net interest payments from 9% to 14% of the budget.

SENATOR,... IF THOSE BOYS ON THE HILL WANT TO SEE SOME **REAL** SOCIAL SPENDING LET'S THROW A BIG PARTY IN MANAGUA!

▲ ▲

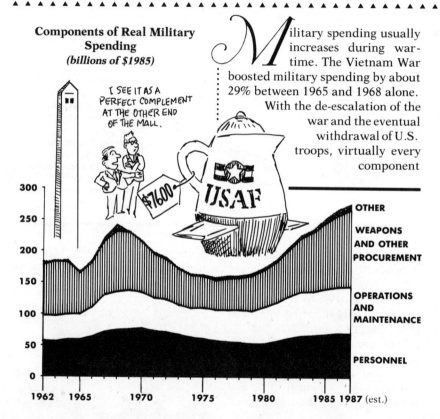

Components of Real Military Spending
(billions of $1985)

300
250
200
150
100
50
0

1962 1965 1970 1975 1980 1985 1987 (est.)

OTHER

WEAPONS AND OTHER PROCUREMENT

OPERATIONS AND MAINTENANCE

PERSONNEL

Military spending usually increases during wartime. The Vietnam War boosted military spending by about 29% between 1965 and 1968 alone. With the de-escalation of the war and the eventual withdrawal of U.S. troops, virtually every component of military spending declined in real terms from 1968 to 1977.

In 1978, however, the greatest peacetime military buildup in U.S. history began. All categories of military spending grew, but expenditures on personnel, operations, and maintenance shrank relative to the military budget as a whole.

The fastest-growing category was weapons and other procurement. In 1980, it accounted for 34% of military spending; by 1987, it accounted for about 43%.

These expenditures are a boon to large corporations in military-related industries. In 1984, the top ten military contractors won over 34% of all military contracts. But the lack of competitive bidding, as well as other problems, led to widely publicized embarrassments, such as the three $7,600 coffeepots purchased by the air force.

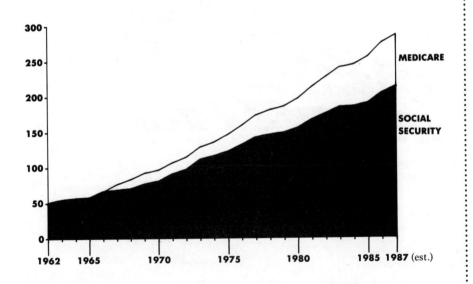

Real Spending on Social Security and Medicare
(billions of $1985)

MEDICARE

SOCIAL
SECURITY

1962 1965   1970   1975   1980   1985 1987 (est.)

*P*overty among the elderly is a problem today, but it was much worse before Social Security was established in 1935. New forms of assistance to the elderly, such as disability payments and medical care insurance, were added in later years, and in 1972, Social Security payments were indexed against inflation.

As the size of the retired population expanded, real federal spending on Social Security and Medicare grew rapidly, doubling in the 1960s and again in the 1970s. Medicare costs also grew because the system gave doctors and hospitals little incentive to cut costs. Unfortunately, some recent changes intended to cut costs have led hospitals to shirk their responsibility to patients with expensive health problems.

SEE ALSO 7.6

6.7 ☐ SOCIAL SPENDING AT A STANDSTILL

▲▲

Steady increases in social spending came to a standstill well before Reagan took office. Modest growth in this category from 1950 accelerated in the late 1960s with the War on Poverty. Since 1974, real social spending has remained relatively constant, while all other main parts of the budget have continued to grow.

Social spending probably would have been cut even further if it had not included many programs beneficial to middle-income families, such as expenditures on education, transportation, communication, natural resources, and agriculture. But spending for domestic programs in fiscal 1986 was about 11% lower than it would have been if pre-Reagan policies had continued.

Furthermore, the looming deficit has made it politically difficult, if not impossible, for Congress to enact any major new social-spending programs.

SEE ALSO 3.12, 7.17, 8.10

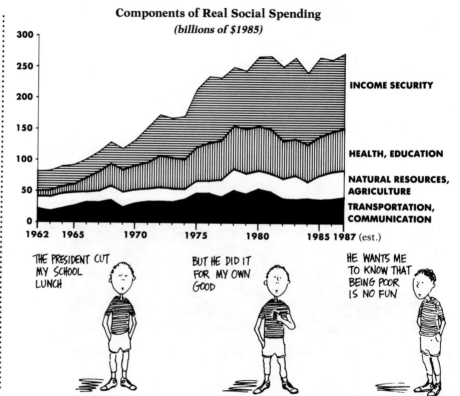

Components of Real Social Spending
(billions of $1985)

INCOME SECURITY

HEALTH, EDUCATION

NATURAL RESOURCES, AGRICULTURE

TRANSPORTATION, COMMUNICATION

1962 1965 1970 1975 1980 1985 1987 (est.)

THE PRESIDENT CUT MY SCHOOL LUNCH

BUT HE DID IT FOR MY OWN GOOD

HE WANTS ME TO KNOW THAT BEING POOR IS NO FUN

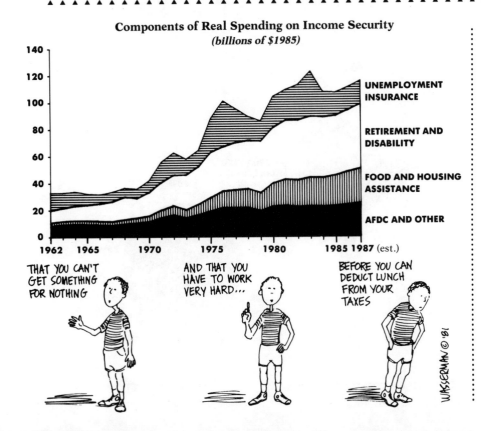

Components of Real Spending on Income Security
(billions of $1985)

UNEMPLOYMENT INSURANCE

RETIREMENT AND DISABILITY

FOOD AND HOUSING ASSISTANCE

AFDC AND OTHER

1962 1965 1970 1975 1980 1985 1987 (est.)

THAT YOU CAN'T GET SOMETHING FOR NOTHING

AND THAT YOU HAVE TO WORK VERY HARD...

BEFORE YOU CAN DEDUCT LUNCH FROM YOUR TAXES

WASSERMAN © '81

The Reagan administration declared a strong commitment to maintaining a "social safety net." But the budgets for federal programs to benefit low-income families proved politically vulnerable.

Some components of income security—such as the retirement-and-disability system for federal employees (separate from Social Security) and unemployment insurance—are not aimed at low-income people. But only those with low incomes qualify for Aid to Families with Dependent Children (AFDC) and food and housing assistance.

Spending on income security as a whole rose after 1981 because of increases in unemployment. By 1984, significant increases in the number of poor people eligible for public assistance increased total outlays for food and housing assistance. But assistance per person from both AFDC programs and food stamps fell significantly in the 1980s.

6.9 □ WHERE TAXES COME FROM

▲▲

The federal government has three major sources of revenue: taxes on personal income (Social Security and income taxes), taxes on corporate income, and taxes on sales and the like. The relative importance of these sources has changed considerably over time. In 1960, taxes on personal income accounted for 53% of all tax revenue. By 1983, that share had increased to 75%.

The changing composition of federal tax revenue reflects a long-term decline in the corporate tax rate and a steady increase in the tax rate on personal income. Even the taxes on corporate income may be largely passed along to consumers in the form of higher prices. Still, they do tend to lower after-tax profits.

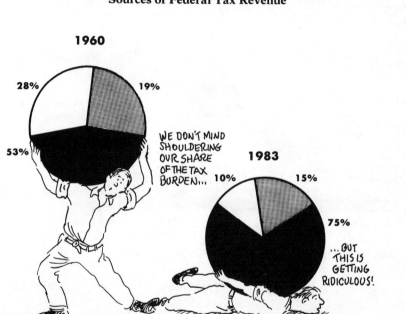

Sources of Federal Tax Revenue

■ TAXES ON PERSONAL INCOME   □ TAXES ON CORPORATE INCOME   ▦ SALES AND OTHER TAXES

Corporate Taxes as a Percentage of Profits

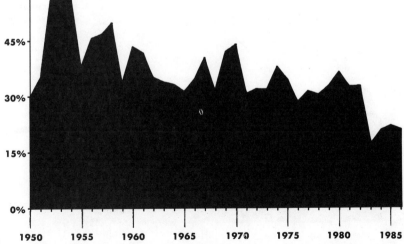

*T*n the 1950s, federal taxes took a big bite out of corporate profits, averaging about 45%. By 1985, that bite had been reduced to more of a nibble, at 21%.

Policymakers hoped that the tax credits and generous depreciation rules they used to reduce corporate taxes would encourage economic growth. Tax credits probably stimulate some investment; nobody knows exactly how much.

But many companies resented the uneven impact these credits had on different industries, and they supported the 1986 tax reforms that eliminated tax credits on investment but lowered the top corporate-tax rate.

The 1986 tax law will probably increase corporate taxes to about the level of the late 1970s.

*H*ow much were taxes cut for individuals in the early 1980s? The 1981 tax cut produced only a small blip in the historical trend toward increased taxes on personal income. In fact, between 1980 and 1986, income taxes plus Social Security taxes averaged about 18% of personal income, far higher than the average for any other decade.

Much of the increasing tax burden is due to Social Security taxes, which rose from about 2% of personal income in 1950 to about 8% in 1985 (compared to an increase in personal income taxes from about 7% to 10%). Families with incomes under the poverty level were particularly hard hit by the increases: in 1978, a poor family of four paid only 4% of its income in Social Security and income taxes; by 1985 they were paying 10.5%.

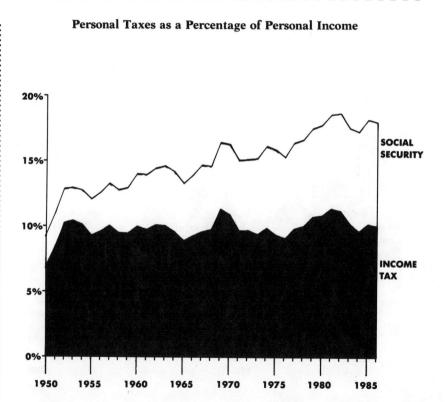

Personal Taxes as a Percentage of Personal Income

SOCIAL SECURITY

INCOME TAX

While the 1981 tax reforms reduced overall tax rates, they actually increased taxes on poor and low-income people. And despite the progressive rate structure designed to tax high-income earners more heavily, loopholes and tax shelters meant that some wealthy individuals paid no taxes at all.

The 1986 tax reform was designed partly to address those problems. The percentage income gains, which won't take full effect until 1988, will be greatest for those who make less than $10,000. High-income earners will gain as well. The top tax rate on individuals will decrease from 50% to 28% (it was 70% when President Reagan took office). But some loopholes will be closed, and a new "minimum tax" will be imposed. As a result, those with income over $200,000 will enjoy only a small percentage tax reduction.

Still, high-income families will save a much larger absolute amount. The 66% tax reduction for those with incomes below $10,000 equals less than $50. The 2% average tax reduction for those who make more than $200,000 amounts to about $2,800.

THESE NEW TAX REFORMS ARE SO BLOODY UNFAIR. I'M BEING FORCED DOWN TO A BMW WHEN I WAS REALLY THINKING PORSCHE.

How Rich and Poor Fare Under the 1986 Tax Bill
(proposed percentage tax cuts, by income group)

INCOME CLASS (In thousands)	CONFERENCE BILL	
	1987	1988
Less than $10	−55.2	−65.7
$10 to $20	−16.4	−22.3
$20 to $30	−10.7	−9.8
$30 to $40	−9.4	−7.7
$40 to $50	−9.7	−9.1
$50 to $75	−0.7	−1.7
$75 to $100	+5.2	−1.0
$100 to $200	+5.6	−2.4
$200 and above	+11.4	−2.3
TOTAL	−1.6	−6.1

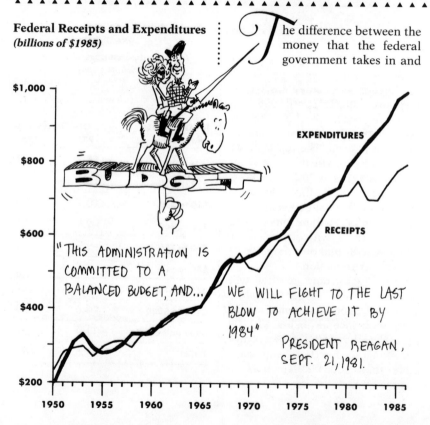

Federal Receipts and Expenditures
(billions of $1985)

EXPENDITURES

RECEIPTS

"THIS ADMINISTRATION IS COMMITTED TO A BALANCED BUDGET, AND... WE WILL FIGHT TO THE LAST BLOW TO ACHIEVE IT BY 1984"

PRESIDENT REAGAN, SEPT. 21, 1981.

$1,000
$800
$600
$400
$200

1950 1955 1960 1965 1970 1975 1980 1985

*T*he difference between the money that the federal government takes in and the money it spends is the deficit. If tax cuts reduce the money taken in while spending continues to grow, increased deficits are inevitable.

From 1950 to the late 1960s, the annual federal budgets show modest deficits or surpluses, with deficits predominating. Since the late 1960s, however, the budgets have registered continued deficits. And the deficits have been getting bigger and bigger, exceeding $200 billion in 1983, 1985, and 1985.

Why didn't anyone predict these huge deficits when the tax cuts were first proposed? Supply-siders were convinced that rapid economic growth would increase taxable income enough to compensate for tax cuts. Unfortunately, the 1981 recession led to a particularly sharp drop in tax receipts.

At least a few policymakers anticipated large deficits but welcomed them as a way of creating pressure to cut social spending.

SEE ALSO 6.5, 6.6, 6.10, 6.11

Increase in the Deficit as Percentage of GNP

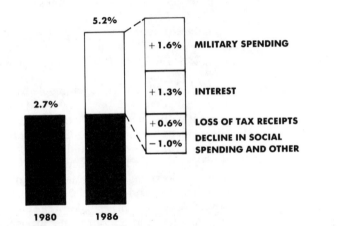

5.2%

+1.6% **MILITARY SPENDING**

+1.3% **INTEREST**

+0.6% **LOSS OF TAX RECEIPTS**

−1.0% **DECLINE IN SOCIAL SPENDING AND OTHER**

2.7%

1980   1986

*T*he ballooning deficits of the 1980s are sometimes blamed on "special-interest" politics or on the public commitment to Social Security. But increased deficits came about for three simple reasons: military spending was increased, corporate and individual income taxes were cut, and interest payments on the national debt increased.

From 1980 to 1986, the deficit increased from 2.7% to 5.2% as a percentage of GNP. Military spending accounted for more than half of this increase, while interest payments accounted for a bit less.

General tax receipts declined, which have added another quarter to the increase. But Social Security taxes grew more than expenditures. Far from contributing to the deficit, the Social Security system helped keep it from increasing further.

"The fundamental test of an economy is its ability to meet the essential human needs of this generation and future generations in an equitable fashion," asserts the Catholic Bishops' Pastoral Letter on the Economy. U.S. scores on this particular test have been dropping. In the past few years income inequality has increased, poverty has intensified, homelessness and hunger have become a glaring problem in major cities.

As Chart 7.1 shows, the median real income of families has remained about the same since the mid-1970s. But the burden of this stagnation has not been equally distributed. Chart 7.2 shows that the share of family income received by the poorest 40% of families declined throughout the 1970s and 1980s.

The number of people living in poverty, depicted in Chart 7.3, has increased dramatically since 1978. Chart 7.4 demonstrates that the incidence of poverty in 1985 was particularly great among people of color, children, and families maintained by women. Even low-income families that managed to stay out of poverty saw their incomes decline between 1981 and 1984, as Chart 7.5 shows. In 1959, poverty was much more widespread among the elderly than among children. But while Social Security lifted many elderly out of poverty, the percentage of children in poverty has increased (see Chart 7.6).

Politicians who blame poverty on laziness are not convincing. As Chart 7.7 shows, a majority of poor people either work or are seeking work. And public assistance doesn't necessarily create dependence. Many people take advantage of it only temporarily, as Chart 7.8 suggests. Furthermore, many eligible people don't apply for it.

Public assistance can reduce poverty. Chart 7.9 shows that the poverty rate is much lower than it would be without government transfers. Existing poverty programs have many problems, but the overall cost of eliminating poverty would not be very high, especially if some of the suggestions noted in Chart 7.10 were implemented.

In housing, education, and health policies, an inverse logic has been at work. Housing costs, illustrated in Chart 7.11, have increased, while housing assistance has been cut. The homelessness described in Chart 7.12 is one result. College costs have increased, and aid to college students has declined (see Chart 7.13). Concern over the quality of education has grown, but teachers' salaries, detailed in Chart 7.14, have remained low.

Health-care costs, documented in Chart 7.15, have gone up, but Chart 7.16 shows that health-insurance coverage has remained inadequate. And new restrictions have limited poor people's access to federal medical assistance (see Chart 7.17).

Chart 7.18 is a reminder that a lot of people in the U.S. don't have enough to eat. They and a lot of other people are getting hungry for some social justice.

7.1 □ FAMILY INCOME HAS DECLINED

▲▲▲

*M*any families are on a treadmill, working harder and harder but barely maintaining their standard of living. The typical U.S. family enjoyed slow but steady increases in income between 1950 and 1970 as wages rose and more married women began bringing home a paycheck.

In the 1970s, median family income began to stagnate, even though women continued to do

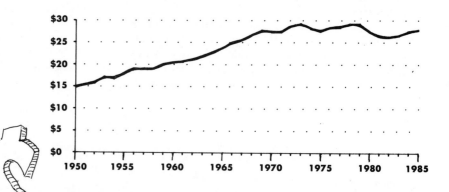

Median Income of Families
(thousands of $1985)

more work outside the home. One factor was that real wages did not grow. Another was a demographic change—more families were maintained by women and more people were living alone.

Between 1979 and 1982, median family income dipped considerably, and though it increased from 1982 to 1985, it has not regained its previous level.

SEE ALSO T.3

Share of Total Family Income Received

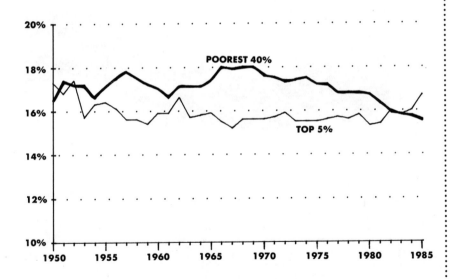

Ever wonder why you never see low-income people in TV advertisements? One reason is that they don't have much money to spend. In 1985, the richest 5% of income recipients, some 5.5 million people, received more of the income generated in the U.S. than the poorest 40%, some 45 million people. That amounted to about $70,000 a year per person for the top 5% and about $16,000 a year for the lower 40%.

Income inequality in the U.S. has increased. In 1985, the lower 40% received a smaller share of income than in any other year since 1950.

SEE ALSO 1.1

▲▲

*P*overty is increasing in the United States. The number of people with incomes under the poverty line tends to rise during recessions and fall during periods of economic growth. But underlying this wavy pattern is a definite upward trend since the late 1970s.

The number of poor diminished in the late 1960s and early 1970s and remained relatively stable until about 1978. After that year, however, high unemployment rates as well as cutbacks in social spending led to sharp increases in the number of poor, which reached an unprecedented level in 1982.

The economic recovery of 1983 lifted a considerable number out of poverty. But in 1985, 33.1 million, or 14% of the population, had been left behind. Despite a higher poverty rate among Hispanics and blacks, about two-thirds of those living in poverty were white.

SEE ALSO 4.6

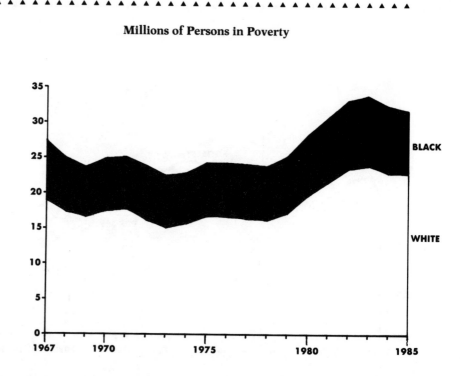

Millions of Persons in Poverty

7.4 ☐ THE LIKELIHOOD OF BEING POOR IN 1985

▲▲

Percentages with Incomes Below the Poverty Level in 1985

PERSONS

- WHITE: 11.4%
- BLACK: 31.3%
- HISPANIC: 29.0%

CHILDREN

- WHITE: 15.9%
- BLACK: 43.4%
- HISPANIC: 39.9%

FAMILIES

- MARRIED COUPLES: 6.7%
- MAINTAINED BY WOMEN: 34.0%

he threat of poverty is far greater for some than for others. While the overall poverty rate in 1985 was about 14%, 31% of all blacks and 29% of Hispanics lived in poverty.

Whatever race or ethnic background, children are far more vulnerable than adults. More than 40% of all black children, and more than a third of all Hispanic children, lived in poverty in 1985.

The type of family a person lives in also affects their vulnerability. Families maintained by women are far more likely to live in poverty than those maintained by a married couple.

I DIDN'T GET A JOB SO I COULD GET OUT OF THE HOUSE. I GOT A JOB SO WE WOULDN'T DROP DOWN INTO THE NEXT QUINTILE!

SAUNDERS

Why? First, the average income level for all families increased hardly at all over the period, while inequality in the distribution of income between families increased.

Secondly, the number of families maintained by women continued to increase, and real public assistance to these families declined.

Many low-income families with children would have fared far worse if large numbers of women had not increased their participation in the labor force.

Certain kinds of work pay off economically, but child-rearing certainly doesn't. Low-income families with children suffered major declines in income between 1981 and 1984. The average income of families in the lowest 20% (or quintile) of the income distribution dropped by more than 33%, while the average income of the next to lowest quintile dropped 13%.

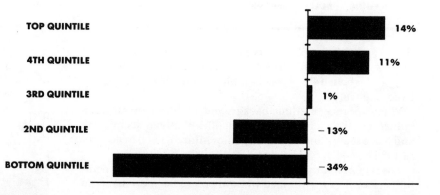

Percentage Change in Real Average Income of Families with Children, 1981–84, by Income Group

Income Group	Percentage Change
TOP QUINTILE	14%
4TH QUINTILE	11%
3RD QUINTILE	1%
2ND QUINTILE	−13%
BOTTOM QUINTILE	−34%

SEE ALSO 4.15

▲ ▲

Many of the elderly remain poor, but as a group they are better off than children, whose overall poverty rate increased from 15% in 1974 to 20% in 1985.

Many children are poor because they live in families that receive little or no financial support from an adult male. And the government is still more reluctant to help these kids out. Unlike Social Security payments, real AFDC benefits have declined in recent years.

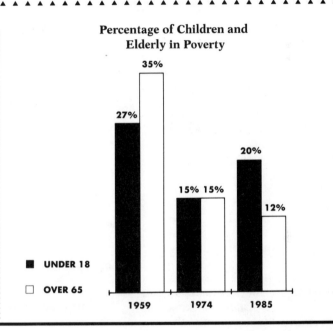

Percentage of Children and Elderly in Poverty

- ■ UNDER 18
- □ OVER 65

Even people unsympathetic to the poor tend to support Social Security, if only because they hope to receive it someday. But many people are not very concerned about other people's kids, particularly those with different racial or ethnic backgrounds. And kids, needless to say, can't vote.

SEE ALSO 3.10, 3.14, 4.16

▲▲

*S*ome people argue that poor people are deadbeats who prefer handouts to working for a living. But in 1984, more than half the householders of poor families had jobs, and 17% worked full-time, the whole year. Another 7% looked for work but were unable to find it, while 20% didn't work because of family responsibilities.

High unemployment rates have made it more difficult for poor people to find jobs. Every budget that President Reagan has submitted to Congress has proposed major cuts in job-training programs.

Changes in federal policy in 1981 sharply increased the rate of taxation on the earnings of those who receive public assistance, making it more "profitable" for many of them to quit their jobs. Relatively few individuals chose to do so.

The Work Experience of Poor Family Householders in 1984

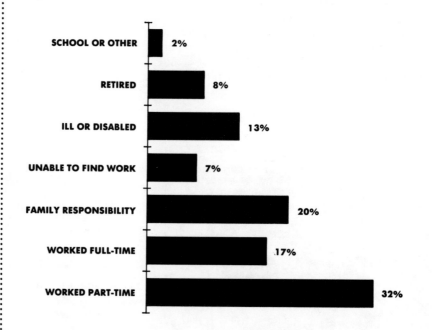

SCHOOL OR OTHER — 2%
RETIRED — 8%
ILL OR DISABLED — 13%
UNABLE TO FIND WORK — 7%
FAMILY RESPONSIBILITY — 20%
WORKED FULL-TIME — 17%
WORKED PART-TIME — 32%

7.8 □ WELFARE DOES NOT CREATE DEPENDENCE

▲▲▲

Families Who Received Any Welfare over the Period 1969–1978
(percentage of all families)

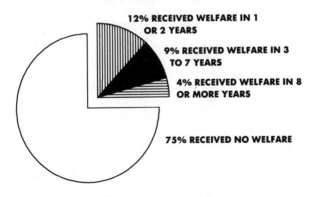

12% RECEIVED WELFARE IN 1 OR 2 YEARS

9% RECEIVED WELFARE IN 3 TO 7 YEARS

4% RECEIVED WELFARE IN 8 OR MORE YEARS

75% RECEIVED NO WELFARE

Critics often speak of public assistance as if it were an addictive drug with permanent side-effects. But one of the few studies of families over a ten-year span shows that it helped many regain their economic health.

Between 1969 and 1978, about a quarter of all U.S. families experienced at least one bout of poverty, and the same percentage received some public assistance. Of these families, 12% received welfare for only one or two years. Only 4% received welfare in eight or more years, most of these with infants.

There may be people living off welfare who could work. But many who qualify for welfare don't apply for it. In 1984 only a third of all poor families received payments; only 43% received food stamps.

By comparison, almost one out of three U.S. citizens received benefits from one or more government programs such as Social Security or veterans' programs in 1983.

▲▲▲

The federal government fought poverty aggressively between 1965 and 1974. Government programs brought a large share of the population up from poverty.

After 1975, however, the government settled for an uneasy truce. As worsening economic conditions set in, public-assistance programs barely held even, and the actual poverty rate increased.

It was not a full-scale retreat, because many programs remained in force. In the absence of any government transfers, the poverty rate would have climbed far above its actual rate of 15% to almost 25% by 1983.

But little progress was made in helping more people escape poverty. And in 1987, social spending for poor people was slated for further cutbacks.

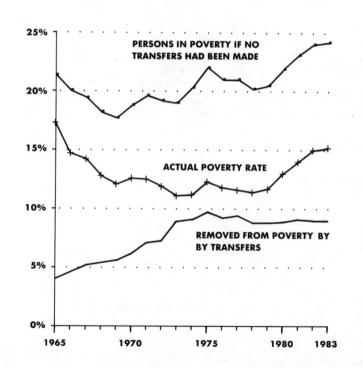

The Effect of Government Transfers on Poverty

PERSONS IN POVERTY IF NO TRANSFERS HAD BEEN MADE

ACTUAL POVERTY RATE

REMOVED FROM POVERTY BY TRANSFERS

7.10 □ THE COST OF ENDING POVERTY

▲▲

The most expensive way to end poverty in the U.S. would be simply to give people enough money every year to lift their incomes over the poverty line. In 1985, as the Census Bureau has calculated, the average poor family would have needed $4,278 in public assistance.

The number of families in poverty that year was 7.46 million. Therefore, an additional income transfer of about $32 billion would have done the job.

How much is $32 billion?

▲▲▲ less than 1% of GNP in 1985
▲▲▲ about 13% of military spending
▲▲▲ about $257 from every employed worker in the U.S.

Poverty could be ended far more cheaply if:

▲▲▲ the unemployment rate were lowered to 4% (because about a third of all poor family householders in 1985 lacked jobs).

▲▲▲ the minimum wage were raised to $5.00 an hour (because 17% of all poor family householders worked full-time in 1985 but didn't earn wages high enough to keep them out of poverty).

▲▲▲ inexpensive high-quality day care were made available (because 20% of all poor family households could not work because of family responsibilities).

▲▲

*H*ome is where the heart is—and where most of the money goes! Between 1970 and 1979, real home prices increased more than 50%, and family income did not keep pace. As a result, fewer people were able to buy homes, and those who did often found themselves mired in debt.

In 1976, the average homeowner spent 24% of family income on the monthly mortgage payment. In 1985, 30% of family income went to the mortgage. Many women sought jobs in order to help meet increasing housing costs.

Many low-income families have a hard time renting, much less buying, decent housing. The average outlay for rent increased from 24% of income in 1976 to 33% in 1982. It dropped only slightly from 1982 to 1984.

The Reagan administration has cut back on virtually every category of federal housing assistance. Between 1981 and 1986, public and low-income housing programs were cut by $17 billion, while the Farmers Home Administration loan programs for people with low and moderate incomes were cut by $1.7 billion.

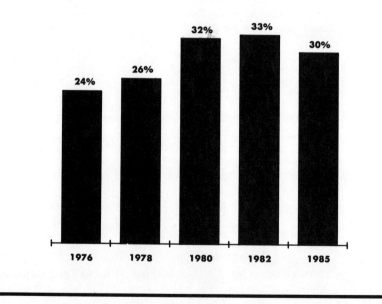

Average Monthly Mortgage Payment as a Percentage of Income

1976	1978	1980	1982	1985
24%	26%	32%	33%	30%

▲▲▲ In May 1984, the Department of Housing and Urban Development estimated that 250,000 to 350,000 people were homeless in the U.S.A., an estimate many critics believe was low.

▲▲▲ In 1984, New York State found that more than 50% of the 20,200 homeless who sought shelter on an average night were parents and their children. The comparable figure for Massachusetts was 75%.

▲▲▲ More than half of twenty-five large cities surveyed in 1985 reported that homeless people were routinely turned away from emergency shelters because there was no room.

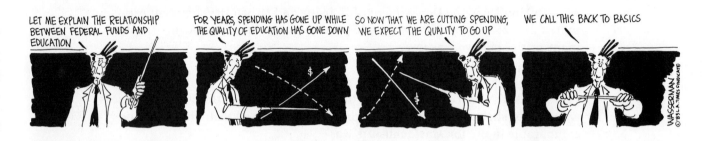

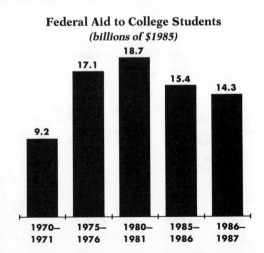

Federal Aid to College Students
(billions of $1985)

The class of 1990 may have to beg and borrow if they want to graduate. Throughout the 1970s, the increasing availability of financial aid made it easier for students to go to college, despite rising tuition costs. Since 1980, however, federal aid to college students has been cut about 24%, from $18.7 billion to $14.3 billion.

The composition of aid has also changed. For the school year beginning fall 1975, outright grants made up about 80% of total aid awarded. By fall 1983, grants accounted for only 48%, and loans had increased to 48%; an increase in loans largely made up the difference.

By 1985, the percentage of blacks and Hispanics among college students had dropped relative to previous years. Further cuts in federal support of higher education have been proposed, and the burden will fall most heavily on low-income families.

SEE ALSO 4.14

▲▲▲▲▲▲▲▲▲▲▲▲▲▲▲▲▲▲▲▲▲▲▲▲▲▲▲▲▲▲▲▲▲▲▲▲▲

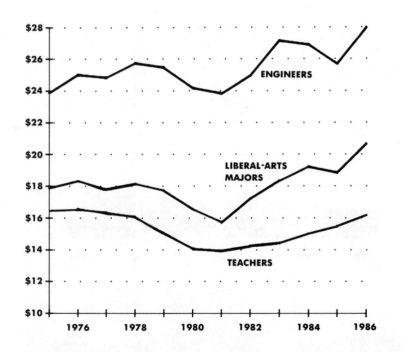

Teachers' Real Starting Salaries
(thousands of $1985)

ENGINEERS

LIBERAL-ARTS
MAJORS

TEACHERS

Recent increases in teachers' salaries have gotten considerable publicity. But those salaries haven't increased enough to compensate for a long-run decline. Real starting salaries for teachers in 1986 remained below what they had been in 1975—at less than $16,200 per year.

Persons with the same amount of schooling but with degrees in engineering entered far better jobs, on average. And liberal-arts majors who entered fields other than teaching earned $2,000 more than teachers.

One of the reasons teachers are paid less is that they work fewer months out of the year. But fewer and fewer people seem to think that summers off are worth the low pay and high stress of the school year.

The desire for higher wages has led to high turnover rates for teachers and made it difficult to attract new talent into teaching.

▲▲

Getting well is getting expensive. The total cost of health care has grown dramatically since 1966, both because new medical technologies are expensive and because our aging population has greater health needs.

Few people can afford to pay directly for their health care. Most rely on "third-party payments" from private insurance companies or the government to doctors or hospitals.

Unfortunately, many people cannot afford health insurance, particularly if they already have serious health problems. And more than half of all households have insurance policies linked to at least one household member's job. If the job is lost, often the insurance is too.

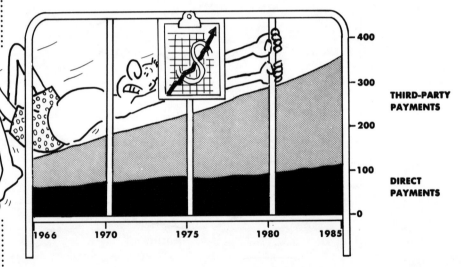

Spending on Personal Health Care by Source of Payment

(billions of $1985)

THIRD-PARTY PAYMENTS

DIRECT PAYMENTS

400 — 300 — 200 — 100 — 0

1966 1970 1975 1980 1985

7.16 □ MANY LACK HEALTH INSURANCE

▲▲▲

Households Covered by Health Insurance in 1985

	COVERED BY PRIVATE HEALTH INSURANCE	RELATED TO CURRENT OR PRIOR EMPLOYMENT OF SELF OR FAMILY MEMBER	NOT COVERED BY PRIVATE OR GOVERNMENT HEALTH INSURANCE
WHITE	79.6%	64.9%	12.4%
BLACK	55.7%	46.2%	19.3%
HISPANIC	55.2%	49.3%	27.0%

*P*eople who don't have health insurance have a hard time paying medical bills. Sometimes thay can't even get the medical treatment they need. In 1985, black and Hispanic households were particularly vulnerable.

A large percentage of households have health insurance that is linked to a job. If they lose the job, they lose the insurance as well.

In 1984, about 60% of children in households maintained by women lacked private health-insurance coverage, compared with 19% of children in married-couple families.

7.17 □ FEWER POOR PEOPLE GET MEDICAID

▲▲

*Y*ou can almost hear a voice say, "I'm sorry, but rule 99X indicates you are too poor to be sick."

Various procedural changes in the past decade have made it more difficult for poor people to prove themselves eligible for Medicaid. As a result, the percentage of those in poverty receiving the aid has diminished considerably.

In 1975, 97% of all poor children received Medicaid. By 1983, however, utilization had dropped to 71%.

In 1984, further policy revisions strictly limited the amount of money the government would reimburse hospitals for treatment of Medicaid patients. Many observers fear that these changes give private hospitals an incentive to turn poor people away.

Medicaid Recipients as a Percentage of the Poor

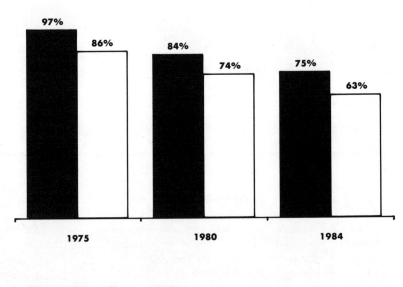

■ CHILDREN   □ ALL PERSONS

7.18 ☐ GOING HUNGRY

▲▲▲ The U.S. Conference of Mayors has reported that the demand for emergency food in 1985 rose an average of 28% in twenty-five cities surveyed. In all but two of those cities there was an increase in the number of families requesting emergency food.

▲▲▲ Sixteen of the cities surveyed had to turn people away from emergency food-assistance programs. Officials estimated that 17% of the demand for food went unmet.

▲▲▲ The Harvard-based Physicians' Task Force on Hunger in America estimates that 20 million Americans went hungry in 1985.

▲▲

From emission controls to containment vessels, from silent spring to nuclear winter, environmental hazards have created a vivid new vocabulary of concern. The conservative response consists of an old refrain: Don't interfere with the marketplace. But the energy sources we now rely on have dangerous side-effects that are not reflected in their prices. And many of the "goods" that are most precious to us—good air, good water, and good health—don't have a price tag on them at all.

Chart 8.1 provides an overview of our primary sources of energy, which are all fossil fuels. Many scientists believe that continued widespread combustion of these fuels will irreversibly change the world climate. Also, the long-run supply of oil, most of which lies outside our borders, is limited. As Chart 8.2 shows, the U.S. and other countries may eventually drink the world dry of oil.

Crude-oil prices, pictured in Chart 8.3, have fallen since 1976. But falling prices are a mixed blessing. They hurt the oil producers we must depend on when prices rise again. Oil imports declined from 1977 to 1985, as Chart 8.11 shows. But imports began to increase in 1986, and if the upward trend continues, the U.S. may become as vulnerable as it was in the early 1970s.

Nuclear power, once heralded as an energy savior, has begun to look like an angel of doom. As Chart 8.5 shows, the U.S. has more than twice as many nuclear power plants as any other country. Safety standards, controversial even in the U.S., are still more lax in other areas of the world. Yet despite greater awareness of the risks, nuclear power has enjoyed the lion's share of the research and development budget of the U.S.

▲ ▲

Department of Energy, as pictured in Chart 8.6.

In the 1970s, a strong grass-roots environmental movement, high oil prices, and innovative federal policies lent considerable momentum to the search for safe, renewable sources of energy. Charts 8.7 and 8.8 suggest that search should be resumed.

A safe environment requires more regulation than we have, not less. Two types of waste pose an immediate health threat: dangerous industrial chemicals that were disposed of improperly and radioactive wastes that have yet to be disposed of at all (see Charts 8.9 and 8.10). Chart 8.11 shows that air pollution remains a serious problem. And a power-plant vinaigrette of nitric and sulfuric acids dissolved in rain water is slowly poisoning lakes and land in some areas. Chart 8.12 points to particularly vulnerable spots in the Northeast.

Regulation has had a positive impact. The clean air and clean water acts of the 1970s imposed environmental standards and stiff fines that forced the cleanup of many major rivers and led to improvements in air quality in many cities (see Charts 8.13 and 8.14).

Economic analyses clearly show that the benefits of environmental regulation can far exceed its costs, and that the price of prevention is lower than the cost of mistakes (see Charts 8.15 and 8.16).

In recent years the federal government has largely abdicated its environmental responsibilities. Chart 8.17 shows that spending on pollution control has dropped, and Chart 8.18 shows that spending on natural resources and the environment has dropped even further.

▲▲▲

Modern industrial economies eat up huge amounts of energy. In the long run, the U.S. energy diet may cause both economic and environmental problems. The biggest slices in the energy-consumption pie are fossil fuels, which are limited in supply, particularly within our borders. Solar power and renewable sources of energy represent little more than a snack.

Burning fossil fuels releases large amounts of carbon dioxide, and the world climate is changing as a result. Many scientists believe that this "greenhouse effect" will lead to melting of polar icecaps, a rise in sea levels, and loss of coastal land.

Nuclear power poses more immediate health risks. Safety concerns have led to the shutdown of many major facilities.

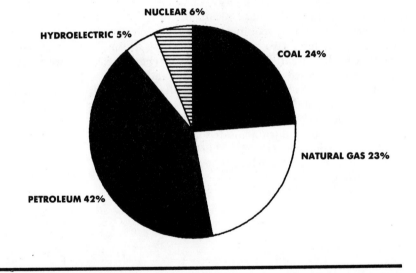

Sources of Energy Consumed in the U.S. in 1985

NUCLEAR 6%

HYDROELECTRIC 5%

COAL 24%

NATURAL GAS 23%

PETROLEUM 42%

Hydroelectric power is really a form of solar power—the sun does the work of evaporation and precipitation that replenishes our rivers. But dams are sometimes environmentally unsound and the hydroelectric capacity of the U.S. is not expected to increase substantially.

8.2 □ A WHOLE LOT OF OIL

▲ ▲

*I*n 1984, the U.S., with less than 6% of the world's population, used 30% of all petroleum consumed, or about 15.7 million barrels per day. That amounts to about 3 gallons per citizen per day.

Total proved petroleum reserves worldwide amounted that year to about 670 billion barrels. At present levels of consumption, that's enough oil to keep the world supplied for about thirty-five years. It seems likely that levels of consumption will increase.

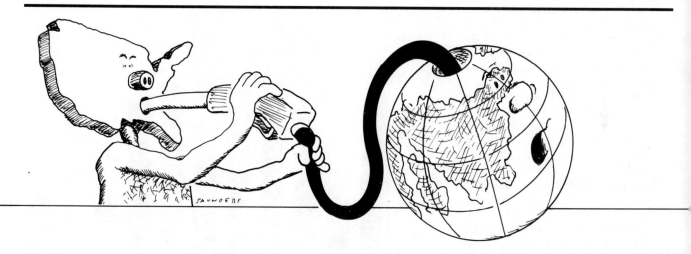

8.3 ☐ OIL PRICES UP AND DOWN

▲▲▲

Oil-price hikes in the mid-1970s and again in 1979 were largely a result of political factors in the Middle East that strengthened the bargaining power of the Organization of Petroleum Exporting Countries (OPEC).

The increases disrupted the global economy, contributing to inflation in the U.S. and the accumulation of debt (to pay for energy imports) in many developing countries.

Most fuel users cheered when oil prices dropped. In the U.S., cheap oil helped keep inflation down in 1985 and 1986.

But the crash in oil prices has also been disruptive. Oil-exporting countries, as well as oil-producing regions of the U.S., have seen their income unexpectedly reduced. In 1986, Mexico began to teeter on the edge of bankruptcy, and Texas and Oklahoma ran into serious economic problems.

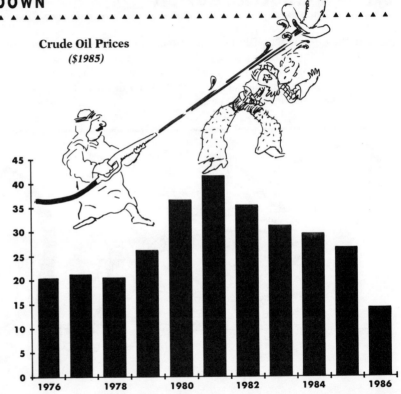

Crude Oil Prices
($1985)

▲ ▲

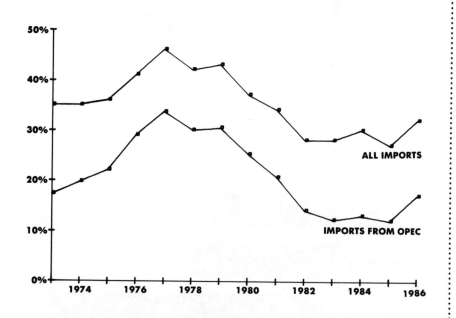

Imports as a Percentage of U.S. Oil Consumption

ALL IMPORTS

IMPORTS FROM OPEC

*T*he spurting price of crude oil provided strong incentives for increasing oil exploration and production in the U.S. and for improving the efficiency of oil use. As a result, the U.S. became far more self-sufficient in oil after 1977. Imports decreased from a high of over 50% of all oil consumed in the U.S. to about 32% in 1985.

Sagging demand for imported oil weakened the bargaining power of OPEC and helped bring prices down. In 1985, OPEC imports accounted for only 11% of U.S. consumption.

But U.S. consumers could be in for a backlash. Price cuts led to increased imports in 1986, and a rise in overall oil use. Many oil executives are convinced that a renewed demand for oil could send prices right back up again.

8.5 □ NUCLEAR POWER AROUND THE WORLD

▲▲

*A*long with the radiation emanating from Chernobyl in April 1986 came new public apprehension about the use of nuclear energy. Because there are no international standards or regulations, it's difficult to assess the relative safety of plants being operated in countries like the Soviet Union, France, and Taiwan.

While the U.S. nuclear industry is better regulated than most, the U.S. also has more nuclear power plants by far than any other country in the world. No new reactors have been planned for years, largely because of their soaring costs. But about fifteen are nearing completion.

The large number of plants increases the probability that at least one will seriously malfunction. According to the U.S. Nuclear Regulatory Commission, there is about a fifty-fifty chance of a meltdown in an American reactor within the next twenty years.

Several European countries have rejected nuclear power. France and Japan, on the other hand, seemed determined to continue down the nuclear path.

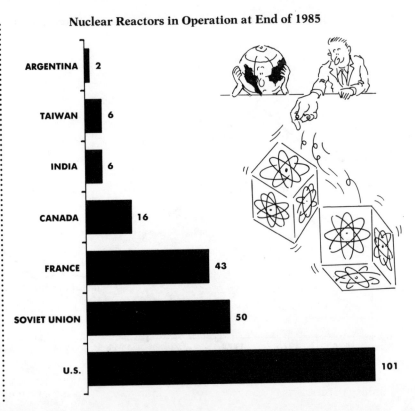

Nuclear Reactors in Operation at End of 1985

Country	Reactors
ARGENTINA	2
TAIWAN	6
INDIA	6
CANADA	16
FRANCE	43
SOVIET UNION	50
U.S.	101

▲ ▲

U.S. Department of Energy Research and Development Budget

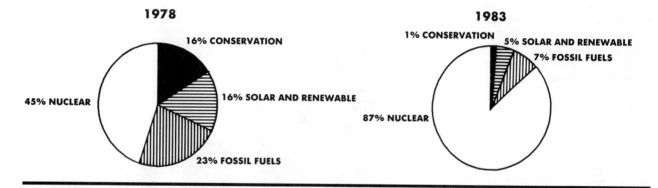

1978

16% CONSERVATION

45% NUCLEAR

16% SOLAR AND RENEWABLE

23% FOSSIL FUELS

1983

1% CONSERVATION

5% SOLAR AND RENEWABLE

7% FOSSIL FUELS

87% NUCLEAR

*N*uclear power in the U.S. has always had Uncle Sam's support. Federal promotion of the civilian use of nuclear power helped justify the increased development and production of nuclear weapons. Without subsidies at almost every stage, and without federally imposed limits on liability in the event of an accident,

no nuclear power plants would ever have been built.

Yet relatively few public funds have been devoted to the development of safe, renewable energy sources, such as solar power. And in recent years federal support for research and development of these technologies has diminished.

In 1978, the Department of

Energy (DOE) devoted about 32% of its research budget to conservation and renewable energy. By 1983, however, budget priorities had been transformed. Conservation and renewables accounted for only 6%, while nuclear power accounted for 87% of DOE research and development funds.

▲ ▲

*T*magine 660 tons of coal. The energy in that pile is equivalent to the energy expended for every million dollars of the GNP.

Greater energy efficiency could help minimize the environmental costs of using fossil fuels and protect against future oil price increases. But despite recent improvements, the U.S. uses more energy per unit of output than almost any other country except the Soviet Union.

Prices have an important impact on energy conservation. Increased oil prices after 1973 helped shrink oil consumption in the U.S. about 33% by 1986. In the Soviet Union, energy prices were controlled, and energy efficiency actually declined in the same period.

But increased prices can't do the job alone. A recent study suggests that government policies significantly increased energy conservation in the U.S. after 1973.

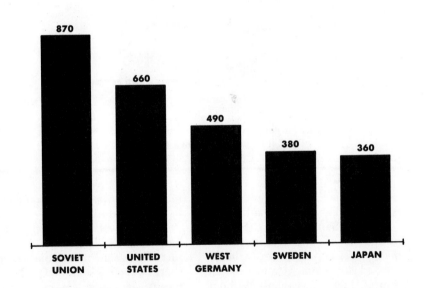

Energy Consumed per Million Dollars of GNP in 1983
(in energy equivalents of metric tons of coal)

SOVIET UNION	UNITED STATES	WEST GERMANY	SWEDEN	JAPAN
870	660	490	380	360

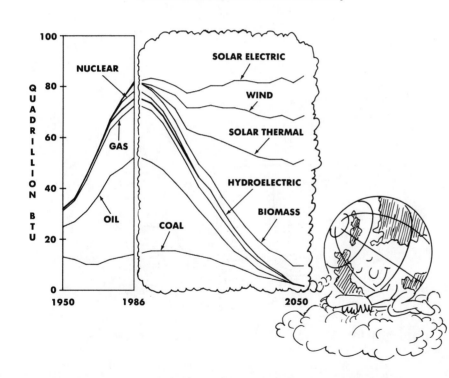

Transitional Path to a Solar Economy

Could the United States economy switch from fossil fuels and nuclear power to safe renewable sources of energy? A sudden change would be enormously expensive. A gradual transition, however, could contribute to economic efficiency and growth.

Transitions in energy use are part of our economic history. Between 1850 and 1900, coal replaced wood as the country's main source of energy. And in the first half of this century, oil largely replaced coal.

According to the Union of Concerned Scientists, much of the technology for a solar-powered economy already exists. Solar heating could eventually support nearly half the country's energy needs.

Falling oil prices have taken much of the wind out of renewable energy's sails. In the long run, though, that wind will probably rise.

8.9 □ HAZARDOUS WASTES NEED CLEANUP

▲▲▲

C*ancer-causing chemicals aren't oozing out of every industrial waste dump in the country, but they are widespread. Many carelessly disposed toxic chemicals leak into underground water supplies where they can never be cleaned up. A 1983 study by the Environmental Protection Agency (EPA) showed that 21% of randomly sampled underground drinking-water supplies were contaminated.*

In 1980, Congress created Superfund, largely financed by a tax on the chemicals industry, to speed the cleanup of hazardous wastes. As of September 1984, a total of 786 sites remained on the priority list for cleanup. More than 10,000 sites might eventually need attention.

Hazardous-Waste Sites on National Priority List in 1984

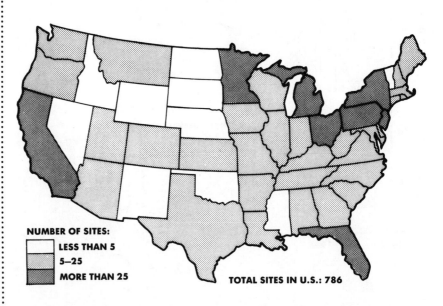

NUMBER OF SITES:

LESS THAN 5

5–25

MORE THAN 25

TOTAL SITES IN U.S.: 786

8.10 □ NUCLEAR WASTES ACCUMULATE

▲▲▲

The Accumulation of Commercially Generated Low-Level Radioactive Wastes
(thousand cubic meters buried)

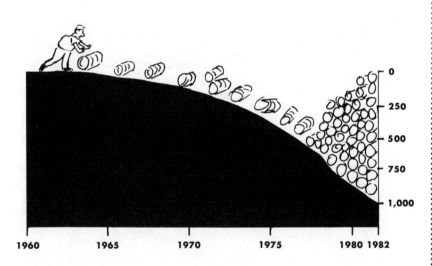

*T*t's a little bit like building and using a toilet before you have a sewage system—only the consequences are far more dangerous.

Both commercial nuclear power plants and military installations have generated nuclear by-products and stored them in "temporary" facilities. Now those storage sites are running out of room, and the government is looking for a permanent disposal site.

Really permanent—because these wastes are so toxic that they must be contained for about 10,000 years.

8.11 ☐ AIR POLLUTION REMAINS A PROBLEM

▲▲▲

*T*he U.S. regulates air pollution more effectively than many other countries. New environmental standards have led to slow but steady reductions in emissions of carbon monoxide and particulates in recent years.

Unfortunately, the amount of sulfur dioxide and nitrogen oxide puffed into the atmosphere every year has not diminished.

Unlike industrial emissions of carbon dioxide, which accumulate in the atmosphere, virtually all the sulfur and nitrogen oxides that go up eventually come down, often in the form of acid rain.

Rain and snow in many industrial areas are now more than ten times as acidic as would be expected in a pollution-free atmosphere.

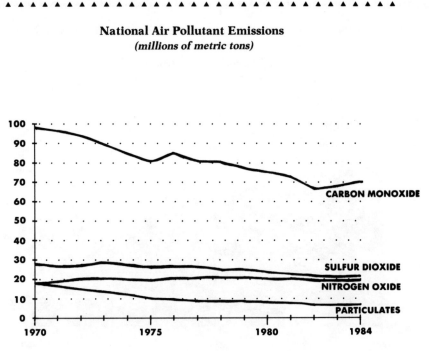

National Air Pollutant Emissions
(millions of metric tons)

8.12 □ THE THREAT OF ACID RAIN

▲ ▲

Acid Rain: Vulnerable Spots in the Northeast
(Based on levels of alkaline substances, which can neutralize acid, in surface waters. Areas with the least alkalinity would be most vulnerable.)

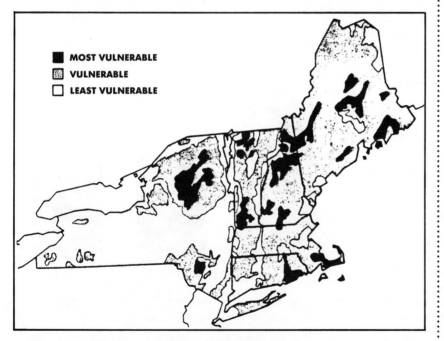

■ MOST VULNERABLE
▒ VULNERABLE
□ LEAST VULNERABLE

Dead trees dominate the landscape of many areas of West Germany and Switzerland, testimony to the long-term effects of acid rain. Will New England's forests suffer the same fate?

Acids released into the air by industrial polluters in the Midwest travel north and east a long way before they return to the ground. In areas where the soil is already somewhat acidic, acid rain threatens fish and may eventually affect trees. According to an EPA study completed in 1984, 20% of the lakes surveyed in the Northeast are already suffering some ill effects.

Many scientists believe that the amount of sulfur and nitrogen oxides emitted from power plants and other sources must be cut in half. Such reduction could cost utilities as much as $6 billion. But the EPA estimates that damage done by acid rain amounts to far more than that every year.

8.13 □ RIVERS AND STREAMS ARE LESS POLLUTED

▲▲

Migratory fish like shad are beginning to return to previously polluted rivers, such as the Connecticut. And many large rivers that were once declared off-limits are now safe to swim in. Between 1972 (when national water-quality standards were first established) and 1978, environmental regulation encouraged widespread cleanup of many rivers and streams.

Still, untreated and poorly treated sewage, along with industrial effluents, remains a major source of water pollution. In 1984, almost a third of all rivers and streams sampled by the EPA failed to meet quality standards. In 1986, President Reagan vetoed a new clean-water bill.

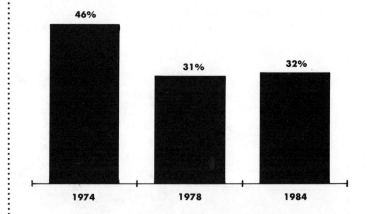

Polluted Rivers and Streams
(percent with bacteria counts in violation of EPA standards)

46% — 1974
31% — 1978
32% — 1984

8.14 □ BETTER AIR IN CITIES

▲ ▲

*W*arning: Breathing may be hazardous to your health. Until new antipollution regulations began to have an impact, New York City and the Los Angeles–Long Beach area occasionally experienced days when it was more than just "very unhealthful" to breathe the air. It was downright hazardous.

The pollution standard index, a measure of the daily concentration of principal air pollutants, is now much less likely to reach dangerously high levels in major cities than when it was first established in 1976. The number of days when urban air is unhealthful has also been reduced, though annually it is still above 50 in New York and a hundred in the Los Angeles–Long Beach area.

Much of the improvement is due to regulations that forced automakers to clean up their act. Strict standards on exhaust emissions reduced carbon monoxide levels, and new auto-fuel standards reduced the amount of lead in urban air.

Number of Days with Pollution Standard Index (PSI) Above 100

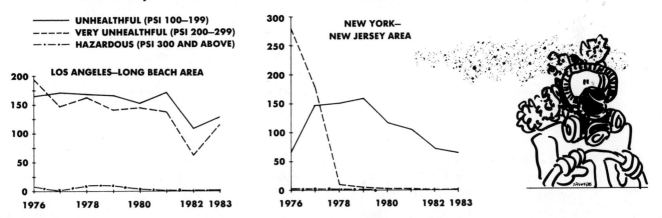

It's difficult to measure with any accuracy the costs and benefits of controlling air and water pollution, but cautious estimates (in 1985 dollars) show the following:

▲▲▲ Reductions in air pollution between 1970 and 1981 provided benefits worth about $33.6 billion annually. Over three-quarters of these benefits were due to improvements in people's health. The cost of controlling air pollution in 1978 amounted to about $25.7 billion. This suggests that the annual benefits of regulation of air pollution far exceed the costs.

▲▲▲ In 1985 $15.8 billion worth of controls on water pollution provided benefits amounting to about $14.6 billion. About one-half of these benefits came from increases in recreational water use. Many economists argue that better regulations could both lower the cost and increase the benefits of water-pollution control.

▲▲▲ Many studies show that poor people are more likely than others to live in urban areas with poor air quality. They are also less likely to enjoy access to clean water for outdoor recreation.

▲ ▲

1986: Chernobyl, Soviet Union. A core meltdown at a large nuclear reactor allowed considerable radiation to escape despite a massive containment vessel. Almost 50,000 people were evacuated. At least 13 people died immediately; about 300 were hospitalized. The long-term effects of radiation exposure will shorten the lives of thousands of others. No one has yet guessed the total cost of the accident, but it far exceeds $665 million, the legal limit placed on liability for damages from a nuclear accident in the U.S.

1984: Bhopal, India. A Union Carbide plant released deadly methyl isocynate into the atmosphere. At least 2,000 people were killed, 50,000 disabled. In February 1985, the company set aside $17.8 million to cover possible legal liabilities, but billions of dollars in damages were being sought.

1979: Three Mile Island, Pennsylvania. A malfunctioning nuclear reactor was brought under control at the last minute. Local residents were traumatized by fear. Controversy continues over the effects of the low-level radiation released. The total cleanup bill (not including the cost of replacement power for the disabled reactor): $1.1 billion—enough to build a new 600 megawatt oil-powered generating plant.

1976: Love Canal, New York. It became apparent that year that industrial chemicals (primarily trichlorophenol) dumped between 1942 and 1953 were leading to abnormally high frequencies of miscarriages, birth defects, and cancer. Studies showed considerable genetic damage among people living close to the dump site. Over 1,300 residents received a combined settlement of $16 billion from the companies responsible. Additional costs of cleanup and relocation are expected to reach $100 million. It has been estimated that proper disposal of the wastes the first time would have cost about $2 million.

Spending on pollution control is an investment in the environment. Unfortunately, businesses don't find such investments very profitable, and the federal government doesn't always find them politically attractive.

Individuals, however, have actually increased their investment in this area. Whenever you buy a new car, you fork over some extra money for emission-control systems that help reduce air pollution.

In 1983, individuals spent almost as much on pollution control as the federal government did. But individuals can't conduct research and development or enforce regulation and monitoring, the two categories of government spending that declined most from 1979 to 1984.

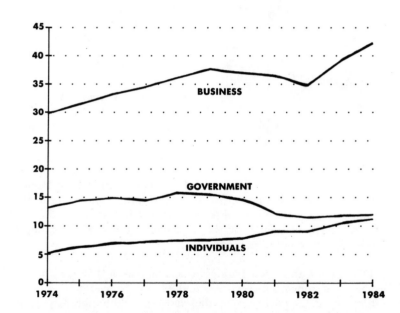

Spending on Pollution Abatement and Control
(billions of $1985)

Federal Spending on Natural Resources and the Environment
(billions of $1985)

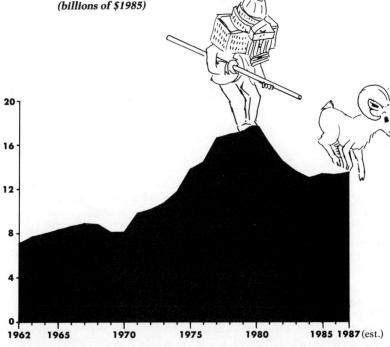

*U*nlike mountain goats and many other animals, Smokey the Bear isn't on the endangered species list. But he may be placed there soon. After many years of steady increase, federal spending on natural resources and the environment was cut sharply in 1981.

Reagan administration policy toward the national parks has concentrated on opening up wilderness areas to oil and gas leasing and cutting back the amount of land under consideration for wilderness designation.

The Environmental Protection Agency has been crippled. In 1981 alone, almost a third of the EPA's staff either left or were fired. Between 1981 and 1983 its total budget was cut 29%, with research funds falling 42%.

SEE ALSO 6.7

conomists call it "macro" for short: "Macroeconomics" is the technical term for the study of the state of the economy as a whole. The main focus of macro is economic growth—increase in the gross national product, or the total value of all the goods and services produced in the country. In recent years, economic growth in the U.S. has slowed. This chapter explains some of the reasons why.

Chart 9.1 illustrates the cyclical nature of economic growth in terms of percentage changes in GNP. During a recession, economic growth is negative. During a recovery, it becomes positive again. The average rate of growth in the U.S. has slowed since the 1970s, partly because recessions have been more frequent.

Recessions lead to higher unemployment rates. And the actual output of goods and services falls far below the economy's potential. Chart 9.2 shows that in recent recessions these trends have been particularly severe.

Sometimes, recessions are unintended. In the early 1980s, however, they were explicitly used to help fight inflation. Chart 9.3 shows the strategy was at least partially successful. But, as can be seen in Chart 9.4, the trade-off between inflation and unemployment is not as simple as it used to be.

Many policymakers argue that the U.S. must simply accept higher rates of unemployment. High unemployment weakens the bargaining power of workers and keeps wages low, as Chart 9.5 demonstrates. Low wages can lead to increased profits, more investment, lower unemployment, and, subsequently, higher wages. But the business cycle doesn't always follow the restorative pattern pictured in Chart 9.6.

Monetary and fiscal policies can influence the business cycle. In recent years, monetary policy has contributed to the high real interest rates traced in Chart 9.7. Chart 9.8 explains the role of the Federal Reserve Bank in this process.

Chart 9.9 provides a short description of the Keynesian logic behind modern fiscal policy. Fiscal policy is largely determined by the size of the federal budget deficit, which affects the demand for goods and services. But the rate of economic growth in turn affects the size of the deficit. Therefore, the best measure of fiscal stimulus is a hypothetical measure: what the deficit would have been if the economy had not been in recession. Chart 9.10 compares actual and adjusted deficits in recent years.

Will current policies restore economic growth and, with it, growth in wages and incomes? Chart 9.11, which documents a downward trend in investment, gives cause for concern, since investment is essential for economic growth. Chart 9.12 shows that increases in the amount a worker can produce in an hour came to a standstill in 1985 and 1986. Labor productivity is as important as real wages in determining labor costs and international competitiveness.

The stock market boomed in the early 1980s, as Chart 9.13 demonstrates. But profit rates, a better indicator of the real health of U.S. industry, stayed relatively low, as can be seen in Chart 9.14. International competition and the high value of the dollar, described in chapter Ten, played an important role.

Prospects for rapid economic growth in the near future are dim. As Chart 9.15 shows, consumers have saved less money in recent years, partly because expected increases in income never materialized. Businesses, as well as government and households, continued to borrow heavily, gambling on the expectation of future economic growth. The increases in net borrowing pictured in 9.16 suggest that the future of the economy rests on that gamble.

▲▲▲

*E*conomists usually assume that more is better. When the value of all the goods and services produced in the U.S. (GNP) goes up, everyone is supposed to benefit. The rate of growth of GNP has been positive in most years since 1950, but its ups and downs reflect a business cycle. Years of rapid expansion are followed by periods of recession (or negative economic growth), followed in turn by economic recovery.

Since 1950 there have been about seven recession years in the U.S. The sharpest dip into negative GNP growth (an actual decline in the GNP) in the postwar period took place in 1981 and 1982. The initial recovery from that recession was rapid, but in 1985 the rate of GNP growth fell.

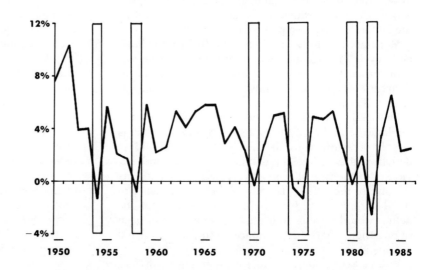

The Rate of Real Gross National Product

□ RECESSION YEARS

SEE ALSO 10.1, T.7

Unemployment Rate
(civilian workers)

**Difference Between Actual and Potential
GNP at 4% Unemployment**
($1985)

1982: $223 BILLION

1980: $120 BILLION

1974–1975: $199 BILLION

1970: $27 BILLION

□ RECESSION YEARS

Recessions are costly. A decline in GNP means that factories lie idle and people can't find work. Without jobs, they can't contribute to GNP. So unemployment can be a cause, as well as a consequence, of economic stagnation.

If unemployment had stayed at 4% in 1970, instead of increasing to 4.8%, GNP could have been $27 billion greater. The higher the unemployment rate, the more potential GNP is wasted. Recent recessions were costly because unemployment soared—in 1982, to 9.5%. Had it been reduced to 4%, GNP could have been at least $223 billion greater, enough to pay the federal budget deficit that year.

*W*hen the economy is booming, it's easier for firms to raise prices, and inflation can result. Even when the higher prices have other causes, recessions can reduce inflation by putting the brakes on economic growth.

Inflation, measured by the annual increase in the consumer price index (the cost of buying a standard "basket" of goods), increased sharply toward the end of the 1960s, partly because of rapid economic growth during that decade. During the recession of 1969 and 1970, inflation began to go back down.

Then in 1974 and again in 1979, oil producers in the Middle East and elsewhere hiked their prices, contributing to sharp increases in the inflation rate.

In the early 1980s, the worldwide recession led to lower oil prices. During the same period, the strong dollar lowered the relative cost of imported goods for U.S. consumers.

Annual Rate of Change in the Consumer Price Index

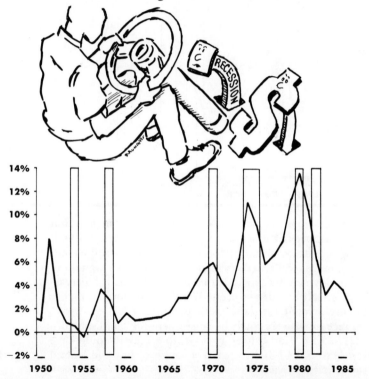

9.4 □ THE TRADE-OFF BETWEEN INFLATION AND UNEMPLOYMENT

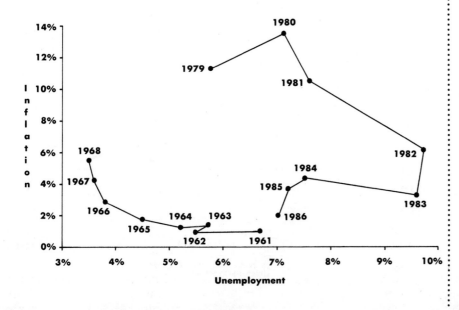

Inflation and Unemployment Rates 1961–1968 and 1979–1986

Greater unemployment doesn't always mean less inflation, or vice-versa. Sometimes there is a close trade-off between the two, but not always.

In the 1960s, the trade-off didn't seem too bad. Inflation increased as unemployment declined. But both rates stayed fairly low.

In the 1970s, the trade-off became haphazard, partly due to outside factors like oil-price rises. In fact, both inflation and unemployment rose in 1979 and 1980.

In 1980, both inflation and unemployment were high. Until 1982, inflation declined at the expense of very high levels of unemployment. From 1984 to 1986 the trade-off disappeared: both rates declined.

But unemployment stayed relatively high. In 1986, the unemployment rate was 7%, while the inflation rate was about 2%. Back in 1965, the same inflation rate was paired with an unemployment rate of only 4.5%.

9.5 ☐ HIGH UNEMPLOYMENT MEANS SLOW WAGE GROWTH

▲▲▲

*I*ndividuals are less likely to ask the boss for a raise if job applicants are knocking on the door. When the unemployment rate goes up, the people hurt most are those who can't find jobs. But even workers with jobs are affected, because the threat of unemployment diminishes their bargaining power. A large pool of unemployed workers—a reserve army of labor— means that workers who go on strike for higher wages are easily replaced.

Of course, many other factors, like productivity and the rate of inflation, affect increases in real wages. But since 1950, as the graph indicates, when unemployment has been high, increases in real wages have been relatively low.

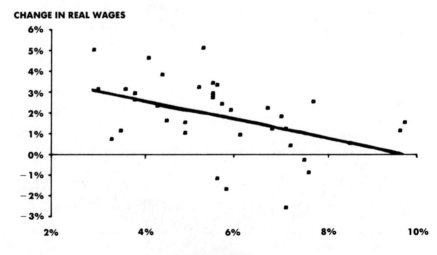

The Relationship Between Unemployment and Changes in Real Wages, 1950–86

▲ ▲

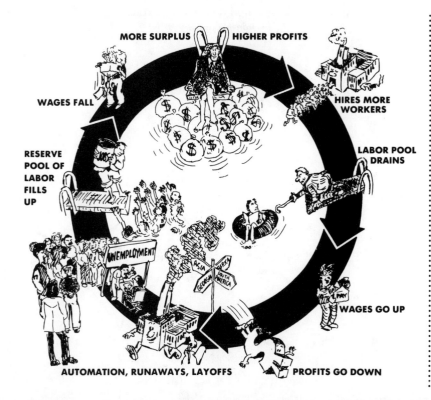

An increase in real wages almost always threatens profits, and the relationship between wages, profits, and unemployment helps explain the business cycle. When profits are high, firms have an incentive to expand and hire more workers. But lower unemployment can eventually lead to higher wages and lower profits.

When profits fall, firms tend to lay off workers, to automate, or to relocate to areas with lower wages. The resulting unemployment may then lower wages and restore profitability and economic growth.

But if wages get too low, for instance, workers can't afford to buy what is produced. Unless demand is increased some other way, a recession can persist.

And increased profits don't necessarily lead to increased economic growth within the U.S. Profits are sometimes invested overseas or invested in ways that don't increase capacity or create jobs.

When corporations consider investing they look at real interest rates, as well as profits. They take the nominal rate of interest quoted by banks and subtract the expected inflation rate, because inflation allows borrowers to repay loans with dollars that have lost some of their value.

In the mid-1970s, inflation was so high that the real interest rate on short-term loans was actually negative. When inflation declined in the early 1980s, the nominal interest rate didn't decline as fast.

Many farmers, small businesses, and developing countries staggered under loans they had taken out under the mistaken assumption that high rates of inflation would persist. High real interest rates during this period also deterred investment and contributed to the deep recession of 1981 and 1982.

Even in 1986, real interest rates remained high by historic standards.

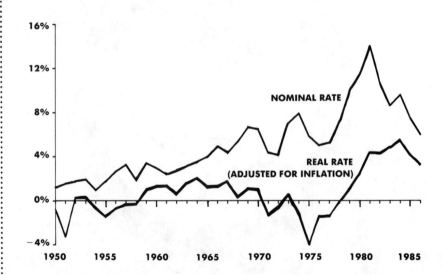

Nominal and Real Interest Rates
(3-month Treasury Bills)

NOMINAL RATE

REAL RATE
(ADJUSTED FOR INFLATION)

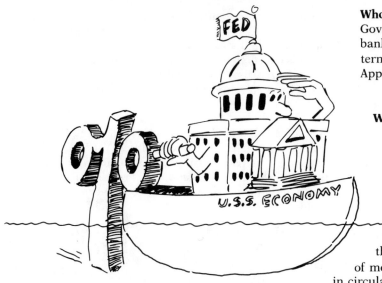

Who determines them? The Fed, a.k.a. the Board of Governors of the Federal Reserve System, a group of bankers appointed by the president for fourteen-year terms. The head of the Fed 1979–87: Paul Volcker. Appointed 1987: Alan Greenspan.

What does the Fed do? It uses interest rates to steer the economy, raising them to induce recessions (as in 1981) and lowering them to encourage economic growth (as in 1986).

How does it do it? The Fed can increase interest rates directly by raising the rate it charges its member banks for loans, called the discount rate. Or it can decrease M1, the supply of money, often measured by the amount of currency in circulation plus checking-account deposits.

Why is the Fed in charge? One reason the Fed steers is that the ups and downs of the business cycle could lead to financial panics or political upheavals if left alone. Another reason is that bankers would rather not have elected officials at the rudder of the economy.

9.9 ☐ KEYS TO KEYNESIAN ECONOMICS

▲▲

Past: John Maynard Keynes (pronounced "canes"; 1883–1946), a British economist whose ideas dominated macroeconomic theory and policy between about 1960 and 1978. Best known for his theory that a lack of demand for goods and services could cause recessions and that deficit spending could stimulate economic growth and lower unemployment. His theory helped explain why President Hoover's efforts to balance the budget in the early 1930s intensified the Great Depression and why the large deficits incurred by President Roosevelt's administration eventually restored economic growth. But Keynes's theory offered few insights into the rapid inflation that flared in the 1970s.

Present: Since the late 1970s, Keynesian economics has been politically out of fashion, and Keynesian emphasis on the demand for goods and services has been largely supplanted by an emphasis on interest rates. Yet U.S. budget deficits reached unprecedented levels in the 1980s, partly because high interest rates slowed economic growth. Huge deficits deserve much of the credit for pulling the economy out of the 1981 recession, and President Reagan is sometimes described as a "closet Keynesian." Keynes's ideas remain influential. While many economists agree that the deficit should be cut, few believe that deficit spending should be prohibited.

Future: In 1985, Congress passed the Balanced Budget and Emergency Deficit Reduction Act, an effort to prohibit deficit spending by requiring a balanced budget by 1991. Since 1985, congressional enthusiasm for enforcing this act has waned.

SEE ALSO 6.13, 6.14

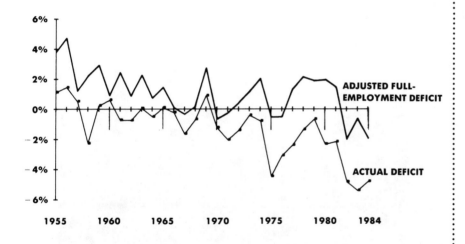

U.S. Budget Deficit as a Percentage of GNP

When is a deficit not a deficit? Like almost every other macroeconomic variable, deficits tend to fluctuate over the business cycle. In recession years, government spending usually increases while government revenues decline, widening the deficit. In other words, deficits can be both cause and effect of the changes in the rate of economic growth.

One way of separating cause from effect is to ask what the deficit would have been if a recession had been avoided. Measured under hypothetical "full-employment" conditions of between 4% and 5% unemployment and adjusted for inflation, the federal budget was actually in surplus during most of the 1970s. The adjusted full-employment deficit became significant only after 1981.

▲▲▲

*T*nvestment is the engine of economic growth. Unfortunately, in recent years this engine has gotten smaller and begun to sputter.

Since the mid-1960s, business investment has decreased relative to the size of the economy. Throughout the early 1980s, investments that actually increased private productive capacity in the U.S. averaged less than 3% of net national product.

The tax cuts implemented by the Reagan administration in 1981 were meant to prod investment. But high interest rates, as well as economic recession, counterbalanced those incentives, and discouraged investment.

In 1984 and 1985, overall investment began to pick up in some sectors of the economy, but not in manufacturing. The engine of growth still needs a tune-up.

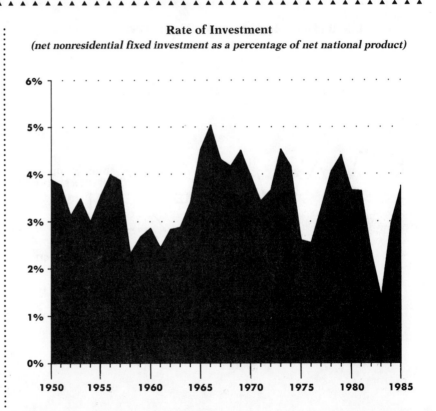

Rate of Investment
(net nonresidential fixed investment as a percentage of net national product)

SEE ALSO 10.2

▲ ▲

Changes in Labor Output per Hour
(business sector)

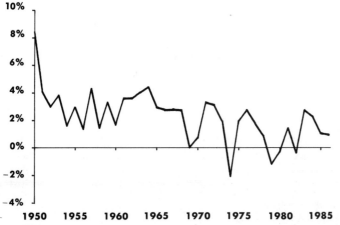

*I*ncreases in output per labor hour—higher productivity—contribute both to economic growth and to higher wages. So it's troubling to see that productivity growth in the U.S. has diminished over time. In 1974, 1979, and 1983, productivity actually declined.

Part of the explanation lies in lower investment. Workers with outdated or inefficient machinery can't be very productive.

Another factor may be poor labor-management relations. Greater worker involvement in production decisions and more job security could help.

SEE ALSO 10.3

▲ ▲

*A*lot of people made a lot of money in the stock market in the first half of the 1980s. The Dow-Jones, a common index of industrial stock prices, just kept going up and up. A wave of hostile take-overs and insider trading kept Wall Street unusually busy. It also made some people unusually rich.

Increases in stock prices reflect optimism about the future of the economy, and sometimes serve as a "leading indicator" of economic trends. But stock prices say little about the actual performance of the economy.

Stock prices began rising in the early 1980s despite relatively low profit rates. As some investors remember, stock prices boomed in the late 1920s, only to crash suddenly on the eve of the Great Depression.

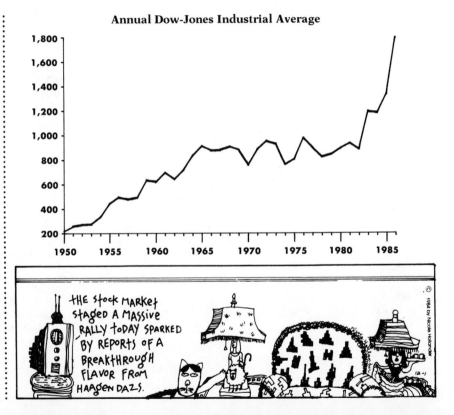

Annual Dow-Jones Industrial Average

▲ ▲

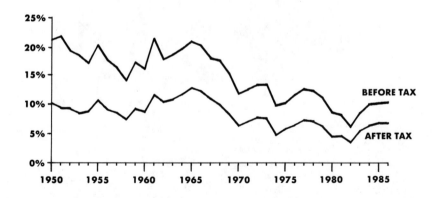

Corporate-Profit Rates
(corporate profits with inventory valuation and capital consumption
adjustments as percent of fixed nonresidential private capital stock)

*T*he profit rate has always had its ups and downs. But since the high-flying 1960s, it has been mostly on the down side.

The before-tax profit rate slid steadily downward in the 1970s. The after-tax profit rate didn't fall as much because of cuts in corporate income taxes. The difference between the two rates was far smaller in 1984 than in 1965.

Events of the 1980s pepped profits up a bit. Oil prices stabilized, inflation subsided, real wages stagnated, and the federal government loosened regulation. But real interest rates remained high and international competition intensified. And while industries supplying goods to the military enjoyed a profit boom, many other industries saw their markets contract and their profits sag.

SEE ALSO 6.10

9.15 □ CONSUMERS SPEND MORE AND SAVE LESS

▲▲▲

*I*n 1980, many supply-side economists argued that tax cuts would increase savings and make more funds available for investment. But despite the lure of high interest rates, consumers seemed less eager than ever to save.

One reason is that saving depends on income as well as interest rates. When incomes go up, people are more likely to set some of their income aside. In recent years, family income has stagnated.

Personal Savings as a Percentage of Disposable Income

I **USED TO** SAVE FOR RAINY DAYS...

...BUT THERE GOT TO BE TOO MANY RAINY DAYS TO **SAVE** FOR.

SO I BEGAN TO SAVE OUT OF A SENSE OF **PATRIOTISM**... LIKE IT WAS GOOD FOR THE ECONOMY. SAVINGS EQUALS CAPITAL THAT CORPORATIONS CAN BORROW...

SEE ALSO 7.1

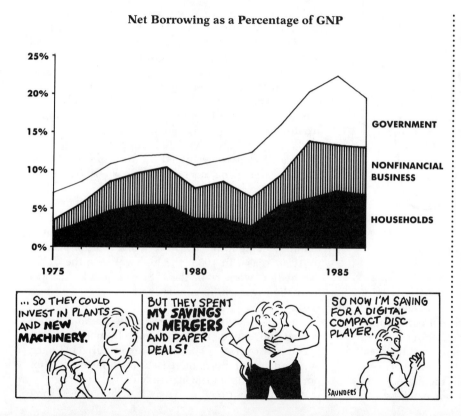

Net Borrowing as a Percentage of GNP

GOVERNMENT

NONFINANCIAL BUSINESS

HOUSEHOLDS

... SO THEY COULD INVEST IN PLANTS AND **NEW MACHINERY.**

BUT THEY SPENT **MY SAVINGS** ON **MERGERS** AND PAPER DEALS!

SO NOW I'M SAVING FOR A DIGITAL COMPACT DISC PLAYER.

SAUNDERS

*O*ur entire economic system runs on credit. Most people know that the government borrows a lot of money to pay for the deficit. But they often forget that households and businesses also rely on deficit spending.

In fact, government borrowing represented a relatively small share of total borrowing until about 1981, when it began to increase at a particularly rapid rate. At about the same time, business borrowing went down, largely because of high real interest rates.

Borrowing isn't necessarily bad for the economy. If the money is invested in productive activities that yield higher returns than the interest due, it's a good thing. But too much borrowing can lead to instability. Borrowers who overestimate their ability to repay their loans can default. And large defaults can have a domino effect, leading to widespread bankruptcics.

▲ ▲

*O*ur neighbors to the north used to complain that when the U.S. sneezed, Canada got pneumonia. Today, countries don't have to be geographical neighbors to affect each other's economic health. Increased world trade offers new opportunities for cooperation, but it also intensifies competition. Many U.S. manufacturers wish that Japanese manufacturers would at least sneeze, if not catch pneu-

monia. And many developing countries are afraid that their economies may never recover from slow growth.

This chapter looks at four aspects of the international economy: global patterns of growth, comparisons between the U.S. economy and its competitors, new trends in trade, and problems of economic development. Chart 10.1 shows that most of the advanced capitalist countries have experienced slower economic growth in the 1980s. Yet some countries have fared better than others. Chart 10.2 suggests that growth rates are largely determined by rates of investment. The fastest-growing economy was the one that invested the most: Japan.

High levels of investment in new equipment dramatically increased the productivity of Japanese workers. Chart 10.3 documents the result of low investment in manufacturing in the U.S.—very low rates of productivity increase. In 1986, the high value of the dollar meant that workers in the U.S. were paid more per hour than workers in competing countries (see Chart 10.4).

The combination of low productivity and a highly valued dollar made it difficult for U.S. manufacturers to compete overseas. The results are pictured in Charts 10.5 and 10.6 Imports increased much faster than exports, leading to a growing trade deficit.

When international trade gets out of balance, some

built-in adjustment mechanisms take effect. As the U.S. trade deficit pulled its balance of payments into the red (see Chart 10.7), dollars flowed out of the country and overseas producers ended up with more dollars than they wanted to spend. As a result, the value of the dollar began to fall relative to other major currencies (see Chart 10.8).

Goods produced in the U.S. gradually became more competitive. But the adjustment process has proven very slow, too slow to help the many companies that have already gone out of business and the many workers who have already lost their jobs.

As the economy has faltered, U.S. corporations have become even more dependent on profits from overseas investment, as Chart 10.9 shows. But this investment has actually declined in recent years (see Chart 10.10). And foreign corporations, many of them Japanese, have increased their investments in this country. By building plants here they can get around tariff barriers and protect themselves from future fluctuations in value of the dollar.

What about the underdeveloped world? As Chart 10.11 shows, growth there has also slowed, with some notable exceptions, such as the People's Republic of China. But even countries as successful as China have a long way to go to close the gaps in per-capita GNP illustrated in Chart 10.12. Not that this is a very good measure of people's real welfare. As Chart 10.13 points out, the benefits of growth aren't always distributed to those who need them most.

U.S. foreign aid could provide substantial assistance to the world's neediest. Instead, it is largely devoted to increasing military and police arsenals that supposedly protect U.S. strategic interests abroad (see Chart 10.14).

U.S. banks have a big stake in the developing world. Chart 10.15 illustrates the rapid build-up of international debt. Slow growth, high interest rates, and increased competition in world trade make it difficult for many countries to repay those debts (see chart 10.16). And debts repaid at the expense of economic development could create even greater debts in the long run.

▲ ▲

Growth Rates in Real Gross National Product

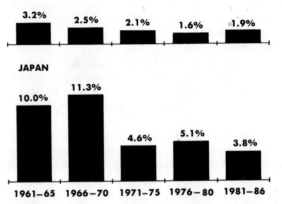

WEST GERMANY

5% 4.2% 2.1% 3.4% 1.5%

UNITED KINGDOM

3.2% 2.5% 2.1% 1.6% 1.9%

UNITED STATES

4.6% 3.0% 2.2% 3.4% 2.5%

1961–65 1966–70 1971–75 1976–80 1981–86

JAPAN

10.0% 11.3% 4.6% 5.1% 3.8%

1961–65 1966–70 1971–75 1976–80 1981–86

The global economy flourished throughout much of the postwar period. In the early 1960s, many industrialized countries grew as fast as 5% per year, with Japan leading the way at 10%.

In the early 1970s, a combination of factors, including increased oil prices, contributed to slower growth in Japan and most of Western Europe. Inflation reached unprecedented levels in many countries and their governments fought it by slowing economic growth. In the early 1980s, high interest rates limited investment and increased unemployment in many countries.

By 1986, many of these problems had receded. But increased competition among the advanced industrial countries made it seem that one could grow rapidly only at the expense of the others.

SEE ALSO 9.1, T.7

▲▲

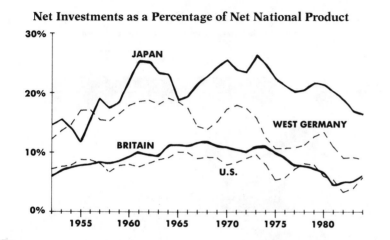

Net Investments as a Percentage of Net National Product

𝓘n the international horse race (or is it rat race?) of economic growth, investment determines success. Small wonder the Japanese have carried home many of the prizes: throughout the 1970s, investment averaged over 20% of Japan's net national product.

Investment in both Britain and the U.S. averaged less than 10% of the net national product in the 1970s, one reason their growth rates were not impressive.

Rates of investment sagged worldwide in the late 1970s. In Japan, Britain, West Germany and the U.S., investment as a percentage of the net national product was lower in 1984 than in 1972.

SEE ALSO 9.11, T.7

10.3 □ IMPROVEMENTS IN PRODUCTIVITY COMPARED

▲ ▲

*I*nternational differences in labor productivity, or output per person-hour, don't have much to do with how hard people work. The important factor is the quantity and quality of the equipment workers use.

Not surprisingly, low rates of investment in the U.S. led to low rates of productivity growth. From 1973 to 1984, the U.S. ranked at the very bottom relative to most of its competitors, with productivity increases of only 2% per year. Japan ranked at the top, with increases of 7.3%.

Improvements in Manufacturing Productivity, 1973–84
(average annual rates of change in output per hour)

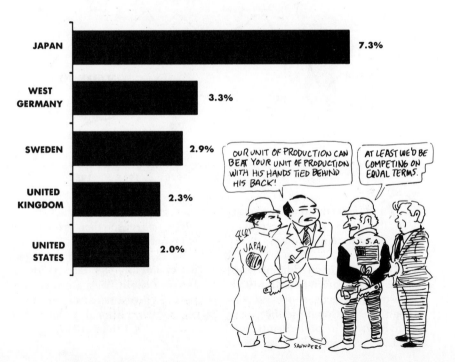

JAPAN	7.3%
WEST GERMANY	3.3%
SWEDEN	2.9%
UNITED KINGDOM	2.3%
UNITED STATES	2.0%

OUR UNIT OF PRODUCTION CAN BEAT YOUR UNIT OF PRODUCTION WITH HIS HANDS TIED BEHIND HIS BACK!

AT LEAST WE'D BE COMPETING ON EQUAL TERMS.

SAUNDERS

SEE ALSO 9.12

Hourly Compensation in U.S. Dollars in 1986
(manufacturing workers)

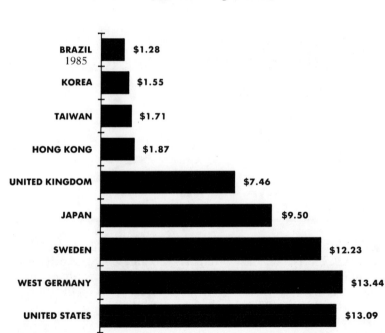

BRAZIL 1985 — $1.28

KOREA — $1.55

TAIWAN — $1.71

HONG KONG — $1.87

UNITED KINGDOM — $7.46

JAPAN — $9.50

SWEDEN — $12.23

WEST GERMANY — $13.44

UNITED STATES — $13.09

What workers get paid depends largely on what country they live in. In developing countries such as Korea and Taiwan, standards of living are low, and government policies discourage unionization. Low wages contribute to the manufacture of relatively low-cost products.

But labor costs are also affected by productivity, which explains why Japan fares so well despite far higher wages than Korea or Taiwan. In terms of output per hour, U.S. workers are still among the most productive in the world.

Currency exchange rates also influence comparative labor costs. In 1983, the U.S. dollar was very expensive relative to other currencies, which made U.S. workers expensive relative to other workers. In 1986, the price of the yen went up, increasing the relative expense of Japanese labor and goods.

SEE ALSO 2.5, 10.8

10.5 □ THE GROWING IMPORTANCE OF TRADE

▲▲

Imports and Exports as a Percentage of U.S. Goods Production

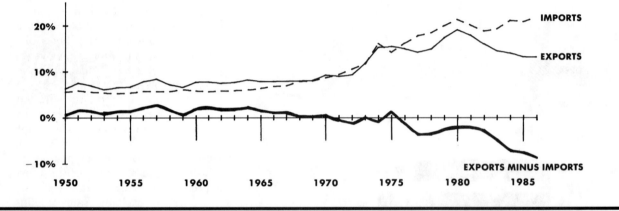

Sony or Saab anyone? Since 1950, U.S. consumers have bought more and more goods made overseas. U.S. producers have also increased their sales to foreign consumers. By 1980, both imports and exports amounted to more than 20% of total U.S. goods production.

Unfortunately, imports grew more rapidly than exports after the mid-1970s, leading to a trade deficit and high unemployment in many U.S. industries. In the early 1980s, the relative value of the dollar went up, lowering the costs of imports and raising the price of U.S. exports.

The dollar began to drop in 1985. Imports became more expensive and exports more competitive. But the immediate impact on the trade deficit was negligible.

SEE ALSO 2.3, 5.7

▲ ▲

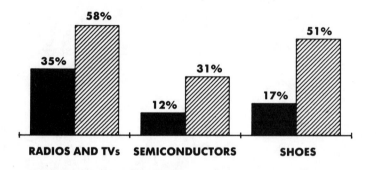

Imports as a Percentage of the U.S. Market

■ 1972
▨ 1984

	RADIOS AND TVs	SEMICONDUCTORS	SHOES
1972	35%	12%	17%
1984	58%	31%	51%

"Made in the U.S.A." is a label consumers seldom see anymore. Producers of shoes and other consumer goods were the first to lose out to international competition. Then foreign brands began to dominate major consumer durables like radios, televisions, and automobiles.

Now more high-tech goods, such as semiconductors, are being imported. Altogether, the trade deficit has probably cost the U.S. more than 1.8 million manufacturing jobs.

Those who favor import tariffs to protect U.S. industries believe that this would only be fair retaliation for unfair trade practices used by some of our competitors. Others oppose protectionism, arguing that it would raise prices in the U.S. and hurt the prospects for increasing exports.

SEE ALSO 2.3

10.7 □ THE IMBALANCE OF PAYMENTS

▲▲▲

*T*he balance-of-payments accounts track dollars as they go in and out of the U.S. One component, merchandise trade, compares money spent on imports with money received for exports. Since 1971 imports have almost always exceeded exports, leading to a trade deficit.

Initially, this deficit was counterbalanced by a surplus from foreign investment—more dollars in the form of interest and profits were coming into the U.S. from banks and overseas investments than were going out.

By 1982, however, these surpluses had declined sharply, allowing the plummeting trade deficit to pull the balance of payments sharply into the red. In short, many more dollars left the country than came in.

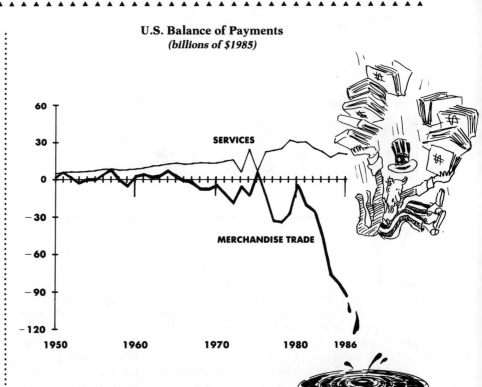

U.S. Balance of Payments
(billions of $1985)

SERVICES

MERCHANDISE TRADE

60

30

0

−30

−60

−90

−120

1950   1960   1970   1980   1986

10.8 □ THE UPS AND DOWNS OF THE DOLLAR

Number of British Pounds to the U.S. Dollar

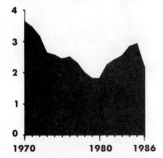

Number of German Marks to the U.S. Dollar

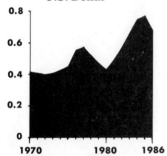

The phrase "strong dollar" has a patriotic ring to it, but a strong dollar doesn't necessarily mean a strong economy. The dollar's value (or strength) is measured by the number of units of a foreign currency it will buy, or in terms of a weighted average of the currencies of all our major trading partners (a trade-weighted index).

By any measure, the value of the dollar fell through the 1970s, then rose until about the middle of 1985. The strong dollar of the early 1980s lowered the price of imports and helped keep inflation down. But it also made U.S. goods difficult to sell overseas, and contributed to the trade deficit.

As foreigners accumulated dollars but didn't buy many U.S. goods, the value of the dollar continued to drop in 1986 and early 1987.

Whether the dollar is strong or weak, high or low, uncertainty about its future value destabilizes world trade.

Number of Japanese Yen to the U.S. Dollar

Trade-Weighted Foreign Currencies Relative to the U.S. Dollar

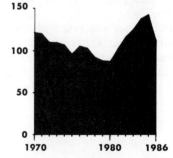

Because U.S. corporations have international portfolios, they have a smaller economic stake in the U.S. than they once did. In 1985, about 30% of all the after-tax profits of U.S. corporations were earned abroad, a substantial increase over earlier years. Profits earned abroad are usually subject to lower tax rates than those earned at home.

U.S. corporations often invest in developing countries to gain access to raw materials (such as oil) or to take advantage of low wages and less workplace and environmental regulation.

But access to markets also influences investment patterns. U.S. corporations invest in many areas, such as Canada and Western Europe, to avoid trade restrictions and sell to wealthier consumers.

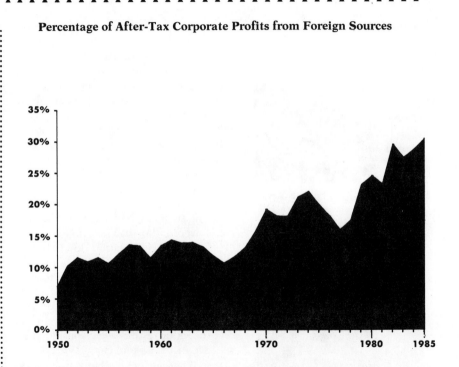

Percentage of After-Tax Corporate Profits from Foreign Sources

SEE ALSO 1.12

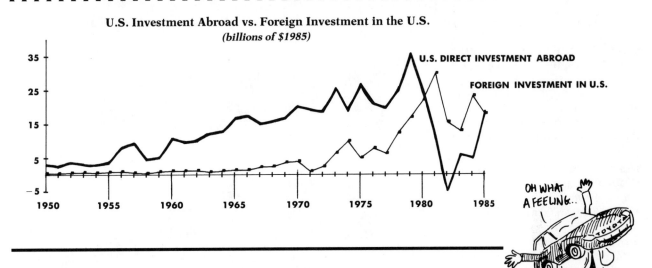

U.S. Investment Abroad vs. Foreign Investment in the U.S.
(billions of $1985)

U.S. DIRECT INVESTMENT ABROAD

FOREIGN INVESTMENT IN U.S.

OH WHAT A FEELING...

TRADE BARRIER

*I*n the late 1970s, foreign investors became gung ho on the U.S., hoping to jump trade barriers, such as auto-import quotas. By 1980, the U.S. had become the largest recipient of direct foreign investment in the world.

In the early 1980s the foreign investment boom continued. Meanwhile, slow economic growth in Europe, as well as political instability in many developing countries, discouraged U.S. corporations from investing overseas.

10.11 □ THE SLOW PACE OF ECONOMIC DEVELOPMENT

▲▲

*D*uring the 1960s, many economists heralded a virtual industrial revolution in the developing world, as overall growth rates averaged more than 6% per year. Since that decade, however, growth has slowed.

In the 1970s, high oil prices stimulated growth in the OPEC countries, while growth in other less-developed countries remained at about 6% per year on average.

In the 1980s, lower oil prices led to recessions in the OPEC countries. At the same time, the worldwide economic stagnation reduced the demand for other exports from the developing world. Higher interest payments increased the burden of debt, and growth in all but the non-OPEC countries slowed to about 2.1% per year.

China alone, of all the developing countries of the world, enjoyed an economic boom in the late 1970s and early 1980s.

SEE ALSO 10.3, T.7

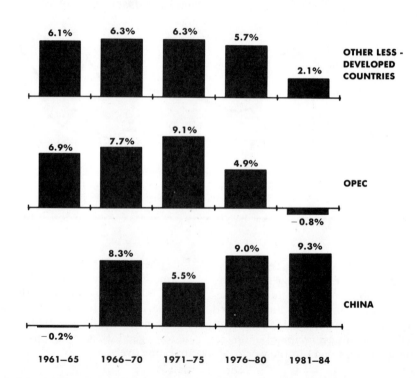

Growth Rates in Real Gross National Product

OTHER LESS-DEVELOPED COUNTRIES: 6.1%, 6.3%, 6.3%, 5.7%, 2.1%

OPEC: 6.9%, 7.7%, 9.1%, 4.9%, −0.8%

CHINA: −0.2%, 8.3%, 5.5%, 9.0%, 9.3%

1961–65   1966–70   1971–75   1976–80   1981–84

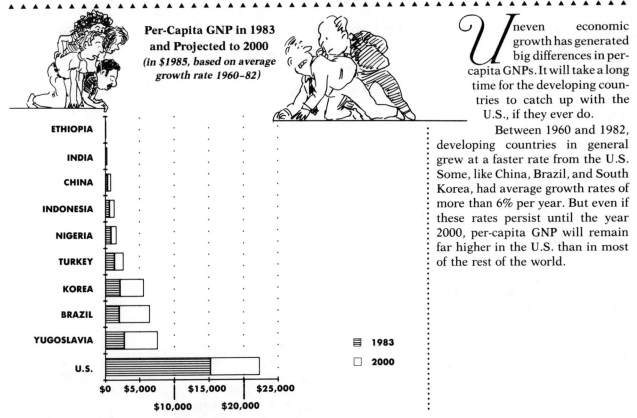

Per-Capita GNP in 1983 and Projected to 2000
(in $1985, based on average growth rate 1960–82)

ETHIOPIA
INDIA
CHINA
INDONESIA
NIGERIA
TURKEY
KOREA
BRAZIL
YUGOSLAVIA
U.S.

$0 $5,000 $15,000 $25,000
$10,000 $20,000

▦ 1983
☐ 2000

*U*neven economic growth has generated big differences in per-capita GNPs. It will take a long time for the developing countries to catch up with the U.S., if they ever do.

Between 1960 and 1982, developing countries in general grew at a faster rate from the U.S. Some, like China, Brazil, and South Korea, had average growth rates of more than 6% per year. But even if these rates persist until the year 2000, per-capita GNP will remain far higher in the U.S. than in most of the rest of the world.

▲▲▲▲ ▲▲▲

$\mathcal{E}$conomic growth helps some of the people all of the time, but its effect on overall social welfare depends on how well its economic benefits are distributed.

Take, for instance, the infant-mortality rate, a basic indicator of social welfare. It records the number of deaths per thousand children under age 1. In general, countries with a high per-capita GNP have a relatively low infant-mortality rate, but political, social, and economic inequalities create many exceptions to the rule.

In South Africa, infant-mortality rates are higher than in neighboring Zimbabwe, despite a far higher per-capita GNP. Cuban infants have a much greater chance of reaching their first birthday than Mexican infants, despite about the same level of per-capita GNP. And China, one of the poorest countries in the world ranked by GNP, provides its infants with a rich chance of survival.

SEE ALSO 4.18

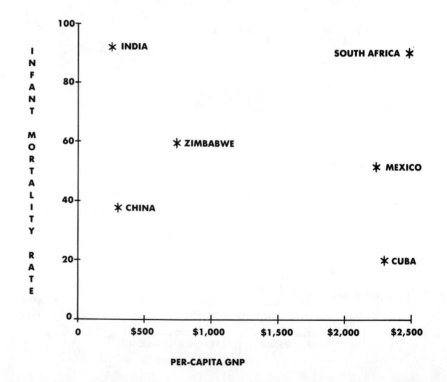

The Relationship Between Per-Capita GNP and Infant Mortality in 1983

The Composition of U.S. Foreign Aid in 1985

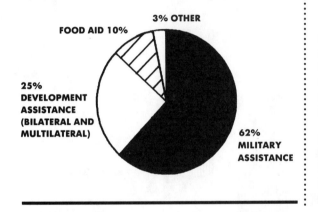

3% OTHER

FOOD AID 10%

25% DEVELOPMENT ASSISTANCE (BILATERAL AND MULTILATERAL)

62% MILITARY ASSISTANCE

The U.S. lavishes aid on foreign military forces. In 1985 about 62% of all foreign aid was devoted to military assistance. Only about 10% went to food aid. About 25% of foreign aid was spent on general development assistance, much of it devoted to financing projects meant to encourage economic development. Some of this aid was bilateral, given directly to other countries, and some was multilateral, funneled through agencies like the World Bank. Most countries that receive development aid from the U.S. are required to spend a portion of it on goods produced here.

The distribution of foreign aid largely reflects U.S. strategic interests. In 1985, Israel was the top recipient, with $2.6 billion. Egypt was a close second, with $2.2 billion, while El Salvador, Pakistan, and Turkey each received more than $500 million. The costs of covert aid, including much of the aid to the Nicaraguan contras, are not included here.

10.15 □ DEVELOPING COUNTRIES ARE DEEPLY IN DEBT

▲▲▲

*I*n 1984, less-developed countries as a whole owed more than $800 billion to creditors in other countries. About half this debt was owed to private sources, mostly banks.

While developing countries on every continent owed money, seven countries accounted for almost half the total debt: Brazil, Mexico, Argentina, Venezuela, South Korea, the Philippines, and Indonesia.

The debt buildup was triggered by the oil price increases of 1973 but soon developed a dynamic all its own. Virtually all the loans were influenced by optimistic expectations of economic growth. As growth slowed and interest rates increased, it began to seem unlikely that the debts could be fully repaid.

U.S. banks have every reason to be nervous. About 10% of all loans held by the largest nine banks in the country in 1984 were made to developing nations.

SEE ALSO 1.11, 9.16

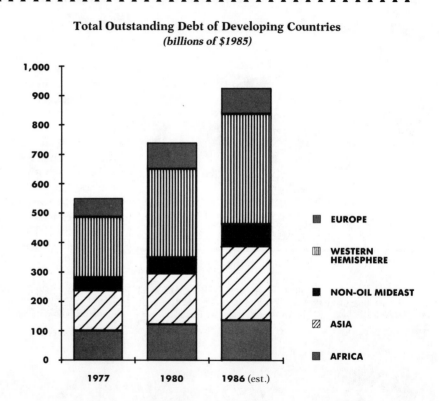

Total Outstanding Debt of Developing Countries
(billions of $1985)

■ EUROPE

▥ WESTERN HEMISPHERE

■ NON-OIL MIDEAST

▨ ASIA

■ AFRICA

10.16 ☐ THE BURDEN OF DEBT COULD SLOW GROWTH

▲ ▲

Debt Service as a Percentage of Exports

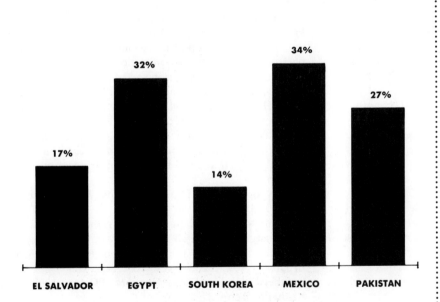

*C*ountries with large debts can run into big trouble if interest rates go up and economic growth slows. Their debt service—interest payments plus scheduled repayments of capital—must be paid in a currency their creditors will accept, such as dollars.

Developing countries can acquire dollars by exporting more than they import, but those dollars are often needed to pay for imports such as oil, food, equipment, and machinery.

Debt service now swallows up a dangerously high percentage of the total value of exports in many deeply indebted countries, and some have been unable to make their payments.

As a result, major creditors like the International Monetary Fund lean heavily on debtor countries to adopt austerity programs to reduce imports.

TOOL KIT

▲▲▲

T.1   A GUIDE TO GENERAL SOURCES

This section provides a guide to useful sources of economic data and analysis. It begins with an overview of general sources, then provides further information for each chapter topic. Use the detailed sources to individual charts in the back of this book to track down or update specific facts and figures.

GENERAL: The two best sources of general economic data are the *Statistical Abstract of the U.S.A.*, published by the U.S. Census Bureau, and the *Economic Report of the President,* published by the President's Council of Economic Advisers. New editions of both are normally available in February from the Government Printing Office, in Washington, D.C.

• Short, interesting, and very useful articles about current economic events are published monthly in *Dollars and Sense,* available from the Economic Affairs Bureau, 38 Union Square, Room 14, Somerville, Mass. 02143. More academic, but still readable articles are published bimonthly in *Challenge* (80 Business Park Drive, Armonk, N.Y. 10504).

•The major publications of the business press, including the *Wall Street Journal, Fortune, Forbes,* and *Barron's* are all useful, but *Business Week* usually offers the most systematic analysis of economic trends.

•For more in-depth reading, the third edition of *The Capitalist System: A Radical Analysis of American Society,* by Richard C. Edwards, Michael Reich, and Thomas E. Weisskopf (Englewood Cliffs, New Jersey: Prentice-Hall, 1986) is a fine anthology of articles in the spirit of critical political economics. A good comparison of distinct interpretations is provided by *Economics: An Introduction to Traditional and Radical Views,* by E.K. Hunt and Howard J. Sherman (New York: Harper and Row, 1985). The Center for Popular Economics has published a detailed critique of President Reagan's economic policies, *The Economic Report of the People* (Boston: South End Press, 1986).

•Some groups that provide workshops in economic literacy are:

Center for Popular Economics, Box 785, Amherst, Mass. 01004

Women for Economic Justice, 145 Tremont St., Room 607, Boston, Mass. 01211

Institute for Labor Education and Research, 853 Broadway, Room 2007, New York, N.Y. 10003

Southern Neighborhoods Network, PO Box 120961, Nashville, Tenn. 37212-0961

Chapter One: Owners. Every October for the past several years, *Forbes* has published a feature article describing the richest four hundred people in the U.S. In late spring or early summer *Fortune* ranks the top industrial corporations of the year and provides considerable information about their performance. In May, *Business Week* usually publishes a list of the highest paid corporate executives.

Chapter Two: Workers. Monthly issues of the Bureau of Labor Statistics' *Employment and Earnings* are the best source of up-to-date information on labor-force participation, industry, occupation, earnings, and unemployment. The January issue publishes annual averages for the preceding year. The bureau also publishes *Monthly Labor Review,* which often includes interesting articles on special topics such as displaced workers.

Chapter Three: Women. A handy guide to economic statistics about women is a recent Census Bureau publication: *Time of Change: 1983 Handbook on Women Workers.* The Coalition on Women and the Budget periodically publishes studies of the impact of proposed federal budget changes on women; it is available from the National Women's Law Center. NW, Washington, D.C. 20036.

Chapter Four: People of Color. The following Census Bureau publications provide particularly useful information: *America's Black Population, 1970 to 1982: A Statistical View* (special publication PI0/POP-83-1), and *Persons of Spanish Origin in the U.S.,* Current Population Reports, Series P-60, no. 27, March 1985. See also in *Population Bulletin:* "Asian Americans:

Growth, Change, and Diversity," vol. 40, no. 4, October 1985, and "U.S. Hispanics: Changing the Face of America," vol. 38, no. 3, June 1983.

Chapter Five: Farmers. The U.S. Department of Agriculture (USDA) publishes a useful book of economic data virtually every year, such as *The 1985 Agricultural Chartbook,* Agriculture Handbook no. 652. Another USDA publication, *Economic Indicators of the Farm Sector,* contains detailed economic data on farms, often broken down into categories by farm size. The Census Bureau publishes *The Farm Population of the U.S.,* series P-27 of the Current Population Report.

Chapter Six: Government Spending. Every January, the president presents a proposed budget to Congress, detailed in *The Budget of the U.S. Government* and summarized in *The Budget in Brief.* The best source for historical data on revenue and taxation is *The U.S. Budget, Historical Tables.* These are all annual publications available from the Government Printing Office in Washington.

Chapter Seven: Welfare, Education, and Health. In March of every year the Census Bureau conducts a survey of U.S. families to determine trends in income and poverty. The results are published annually in the Current Population Reports, series P-60, often under the title *Money Income of Households, Families, and Persons in the United States.* Recently, the bureau began to conduct a survey to determine who receives public assistance. Some of the results are published quarterly in the Current Population Reports, series P-70, *Economic Characteristics of Households in the United States.* Expenditures per recipient in social programs such as Aid to Families with Dependent Children are published monthly in *Social Security Bulletin,* published by the Social Security Administration.

Chapter Eight: Energy and the Environment. One of the best sources of up-to-date information on energy prices and consumption is *Monthly Energy Review,* published by the Energy Information Administration of the Department of Energy. *Environmental Quality,* the annual report of the President's Council on Environmental Quality, is an excellent source of historical data on environmental problems. It was discontinued in 1985. Good technical information is presented in *State of the Environment: An Assesment at Mid-Decade,* published by the Conservation Foundation, Washington D.C., 1984.

Chapter Nine: Macroeconomics. The tables published in the back of the *Economic Report of the President,* described above under general sources, are an excellent source of summary statistics. Tables in the monthly *Survey of Current Business,* published by the Department of Commerce, and the *Federal Reserve Bulletin,* published by the Federal Reserve Bank, provide even more up-to-date data.

Chapter Ten: The Global Economy. The May issue of the Commerce Department's *Survey of Current Business* summarizes U.S. international transactions for the preceding year. The *Federal Reserve Bulletin* also includes a great deal of data on foreign trade and foreign exchange rates. The *World Development Report,* published annually by the World Bank in Washington, D.C., provides useful tables describing many aspects of economic development.

T.2 HOW TO READ AND WRITE GRAPHS

Although we are bombarded daily by graphs and charts, it's easy to be intimidated, confused, or misled by them. Along with remembering some basic guidelines, the best way to learn to read graphs is to make a few. Once you can make them by hand, you might have the inclination and the opportunity to take advantage of modern computer software that allows you to punch them out with abandon.

Here are some basic guidelines:

1. Figure out what the variables are. A graph usually displays a relationship between the values of two or more variables. In bar-and-line graphs, the value of one variable is usually represented on a horizontal axis that starts with the smallest value and increases to the right. The values of other variables are usually represented on a vertical axis that starts at zero and increases upward. For instance, look at Chart 2.5. Along the horizontal axis, time increases from 1950 to 1986; along the vertical axis, the value of earnings increases from $0 to $10. Pie charts usually picture the relationship between a whole and its parts (see Chart 5.3). Columns or bars can be used the same way (see Chart 3.9).

2. Look at the range of the values of the variables:Sometimes they start at a higher value than zero (see Chart 3.13). Sometimes they are multiples of numbers, such as thousands or millions (see Chart 1.13). The scale of measurement used largely determines the visual impact of a graph.

3. Ask yourself what you expected the relationship to be. Graphs display patterns. Only a critical, attentive reader can decide whether those patterns really represent trends or explanations.

When you set out to make graphs, follow a similar line of reasoning:

1. Choose the variables whose relationship you want to explore or display, and let this determine the type of graph.

2. Decide on the range and the units you want to use. Experiment with some alternatives; this is a trial-and-error process.

3. Choose the size of your horizontal and vertical axes, or the diameter of your pie. Pick a size that is practical, one that allows enough space to show the variation you want to show. Be aware that the relative size of the two axes will determine the relative variation in the two variables. If the vertical axis is very long relative to the horizontal axis, the values will show more vertical variation.

4. For bar-and-line graphs, mark off the values on the vertical and horizontal axes, so you have a grid. Then plot your values on the grid. For pie graphs, divide the size of the part into the size of the whole, and calculate the number of degrees in an angle that bears the same relationship to 360 (the size of the whole circle in degrees). This will determine the size of the wedge.

5. Compare the results with your expectations, and ask yourself if the pattern is consistent with your explanation.

A computer can do much of the trial-and-error part of this work—though you still have to make the decisions and enter the numbers. The specifics depend almost entirely on the type of computer facilities you have access to. In general:

1. You need access to a computer, a printer or plotter, and some software that are explicitly designed to draw graphs and charts. Any local computer facility or store should be able to help you.

2. Unless you can get assistance from an experienced person, be prepared to invest a fair amount of time

familiarizing yourself with the equipment and software. In general, the more "powerful" a graphing program is, or the greater number of fancy things it can do, the more time it takes to learn how to use it.
3. If you are going to generate a lot of graphs with a lot of numbers, it's helpful to use a graphing program that is compatible with what is called a spreadsheet—a program that allows you to add, subtract, multiply, and divide rows and columns of numbers and then transfer them directly into the graphing program.

T.3 MEANS, MEDIANS, AND OTHER MEASURES

Sometimes empirical data is wrapped up in a bewildering variety of statistical terms, such as means and medians. You can look up their definitions in a dictionary or glossary, but the best way to learn what they mean is to apply them yourself.

In order to summarize information about a large number of cases, ask what's happening to the "typical" case. There are two common but different ways of defining "typical."

The simplest and most common way is to calculate the *average* (sometimes called the *mean*). For instance, if you want to know the income of the typical U.S. family, you can take the sum of all family income and divide it by the number of families. Another way to define "typical" is by the *median*. You can find the median by lining up all the relevant cases from the lowest value to the highest and choosing the one that is exactly in the middle. This would show, for instance, which family's income was greater than 50% of all families and less than the other 50%.

Sometimes the average and the median are the same. More often, they diverge. The reason is that extreme cases affect the average more than the median. For instance if you added one family with an income 100 times greater than the next family it would pull the average up a great deal but change the median hardly at all. The overall distribution of income, like the distribution of both earnings and wealth, has many more extreme cases on the high side than on the low side. For this reason, the average vastly overestimates the income of the typical family, and the median is a better measure.

T.4 THE REAL VERSUS THE NOMINAL: HOW TO USE PRICE INDICES

Most people think that something that is real is simply something that is not imaginary. In the economist's world, however, the word *real* describes a number that has been adjusted to take account of inflation. A *real value* is one that is expressed in *constant dollars*—dollars with the same purchasing power.

The opposite of a real value is a *nominal value:* it

reflects the *current* value, the purchasing power the dollar had in that year.

You can use estimates of the rate of inflation to convert nominal values to real values. First, you must decide what estimate of the rate of inflation to use. The most commonly used measure is the *consumer price index* (CPI). This index calculates the cost of a certain basket of goods (including food, clothing, and housing) in a certain benchmark year and determines how many dollars would have been required in another year to purchase the same basket. The ratio between the two determines the CPI.

For instance, in 1985 the CPI was 322.2, relative to the benchmark year 1967, which is set at 100. That means that $3.22 in 1985 had the same purchasing power as $1.00 in 1967. To calculate how much larger your 1985 salary of $18,000 was in real terms compared to 1967, you would calculate as follows:

$$\frac{1985 \text{ CPI:}}{1967 \text{ CPI:}} = \frac{\text{your salary in 1985 dollars}}{\text{your salary in 1967 dollars}}$$

$$\frac{322.2}{100} = \frac{\$18,000}{X}$$

Using a little algebra ("cross-multiply and divide"— multiply the 1967 CPI by the 1985 salary, then divide by the 1985 CPI), you can determine that if you earned $5,586.59 in 1967 you would have been able to buy about what you can buy today with your current salary.

Compare that to what you actually earned in 1967.

What if you weren't earning a living—or even alive—in 1967? Just because 1967 is commonly used as the benchmark year for published statistics doesn't mean you have to use 1967 dollars. As long as you can consult an estimate of the CPI for the range of years you are interested in, you can use any year as a base year. Say you want to compare your real earnings of 1980 and 1985. The 1980 CPI is 246.8. You can use the figure you just used for 1985 CPI to convert your 1985 salary (say, $18,000 again) to 1980 dollars as follows:

$$\frac{322.2}{246.8} = \frac{\$18,000}{X}$$

A few calculations show that X, your 1985 salary in $1980, is $13,787.70. Did you earn more or less than that in 1980?

The consumer price index is not a perfect measure of the purchasing power of your dollars, because the goods and services you spend your money on may be quite different from those included in the basket of goods that the Bureau of Labor Statistics uses. Another complication is that the composition of the average basket of goods that people do buy varies over time. The rates of price increase vary considerably; in some years, food prices may increase faster—and in other years, slower—than the cost of other commodities. In addition to the CPI, based on the whole market basket, the bureau publishes indices for many individual items.

Many important economic data, such as measurements of the *gross national product* or of investment, pertain to sums of money that are not really spent by consumers. To convert these sums to real terms, you would use a different index, the *implicit price deflator,* which is calculated for this purpose. You can use it exactly the same way as the CPI, using either the overall index or the index of any of its separate components.

T.5 THE CENSUS VOCABULARY: FAMILIES, HOUSEHOLDS, PERSONS, AND HEADS

In the language of the Census Bureau, a *person* is just what the word sounds like—an individual human being. The official bureau terms *families* and *households,* however, mean something a little different from ordinary language. A *family* is any group of people related by blood, marriage, or adoption living at the same residence. If you don't live with your parents, you are not considered part of their family (and your income is not considered part of their family income). People who live alone are not considered members of families. By official definition, they represent single-person households.

A *household* consists of all the people living in one residence, whether or not they are related. Individuals, unrelated roommates, and families all qualify, but people living in "institutions" such as prisons, army barracks, hospitals, and homes for the elderly are not considered part of households. Here's one way to keep the distinction straight: According to the Census Bureau, all families are households but not all households are families.

People who compile statistics should choose their units of analysis carefully. Sometimes the problems are obvious. You wouldn't want to ask what percentage of households have experienced a divorce, because many household members aren't even married. You also wouldn't want to ask what percentage of families received Social Security, because you would be excluding all people living alone, many of whom are elderly.

At other times, the problems are not so obvious. The percentage of all households that include children is arguably just as interesting a fact as the percentage of families that include children. But the two percentages mean different things and should not be confused.

Beyond the distinction between household and family lies the question of "headship." Until 1980, the bureau always classified a husband as the *head* of his family if he lived in the same household. A female-headed family household was, by definition, a family household lacking a husband. Now, the bureau is more diplomatic, and designates the person in whose name the home is owned or rented as the *householder.* If the home is owned or rented jointly by a married couple, either the husband or wife may be the householder. The families once termed "female-headed" are now termed "families with female householders, no husband present." The Bureau of Labor Statistics has a nicer way of putting it: "families maintained by women."

T.6 WHAT THEY CALL US: RACIAL AND ETHNIC LABELS IN ECONOMIC DATA

Everyone who works with economic statistics about people should pay attention to the implications of racial and ethnic labels. The categories that government agencies such as the Census Bureau and the Bureau of Labor Statistics use to define and gather economic data reflect the unspoken assumptions and biases of the larger society. Sometimes these categories are politically offensive or simply outdated. Sometimes agencies change and improve the racial and ethnic labels. However welcome, such changes make it difficult to compare data collected in different years.

Take, for instance, the category *nonwhite,* which government agencies used until recently to describe blacks, Asians, and Native Americans as a group. This term accurately reflected conventional English usage before the 1970s, a usage defined by a white population that automatically considered its own race as the stan-

dard. It's a bit analogous to defining women as "non-men."

The conventional racial categories *white* and *nonwhite* also overlooked the distinctive character and sense of community shared by people whose ethnic origins lay in Spanish-speaking countries. In 1979 many government agencies responded to widespread criticism by changing their categories to *white, black,* and *Hispanic* (of Spanish origin), providing data for these three groups and largely discontinuing the white-nonwhite distinction. This change unfortunately makes it difficult to construct long-run data series. There is no data predating 1978 for blacks and Hispanics as separate groups, and there is very little data after 1978 for Asians, Native Americans, or people of color as a whole.

It is easy to overlook the implications of these distinctions. For instance, you might think that you could arrive at the total number of families in poverty by adding together the white, black, and Hispanic families in poverty. Not so. Hispanic is an ethnic, not a racial, designation. Hispanics can be either black or white, and if you add their numbers to the numbers of black and white families, you will overcount the total. Furthermore, you will overlook the Asian and Native American families that live in poverty.

For the most part, the Census Bureau invites people to define their own race and ethnicity, and there are no hard-and-fast rules for people to follow. For instance, after 1970, American Indians became more assertive of their cultural pride and political rights, and by 1980 many people who had never done so before identified themselves as Indians. If you didn't know this, you might infer incorrectly from Census Bureau publications that American Indians had an extraordinarily high rate of population growth.

It is sometimes tempting to splice two data series together—say, joining a series on average earnings for nonwhites with a later series for blacks, reasoning that blacks, after all, are by far the largest group in the category. But the inaccuracy would not be negligible. For instance, people of Asian origin, though small in numbers in the 1970s, had relatively high incomes; including them in the nonwhite category would raise the average earnings of nonwhites significantly above the average earnings of blacks.

No matter how careful you are, you still have to make difficult decisions about how to categorize groups of people. Here are some of the decisions we have made:
1. Wherever feasible, we break numbers into detailed racial and ethnic categories.
2. Because we think there is an important political and cultural boundary between whites and a group that includes blacks, Hispanics, Asians, and Native Americans, we use the term *people of color* as an alternative to *nonwhite*. It is an alternative, not a synonym, because it includes Hispanics, which "nonwhite" does not.

3. We follow the current Bureau of Labor Statistics practice of using the term *Hispanic* for people who identify themselves as being of Spanish origin, although we recognize that the term *Latino* is preferred by many, particularly in the western states.
4. We use the term *Native Americans* to refer to the group the Census Bureau labels *American Indians, Eskimos, and Aleuts.*

T.7 MEASURING GROWTH: WHAT'S GROSS ABOUT GROSS NATIONAL PRODUCT?

When economists use the word *gross* they usually mean "total." The *Gross national product* (GNP) is simply the total value of all the goods and services produced for sale within a country (usually in a given year). But there is something a little gross, even downright vulgar, about using the GNP as a measure of total production or economic welfare. The many goods and services produced in households are not included in the GNP, because they aren't sold. And the GNP doesn't reflect changes in the quantity or quality of goods that don't have a price tag, like clean air or good health.

But unless and until a better summary of production is widely adopted, the GNP will remain central to the national income accounts that government agencies use to track the growth of the economy. Most other important accounting categories are subsets of the GNP. For instance, the *Net national product* (NNP) is the GNP minus the value of capital goods used up either in the process of production or through depreciation. In national accounts, depreciation is synonymous with *capital consumption allowances.*

The national accounts break the GNP down into four components:

1. Goods and services bought by households and individuals, or *personal consumption expenditures.*
2. Those bought by businesses, i.e., *gross private domestic investment,* including investment in inventory.
3. Exports minus imports, or *net exports* (negative in recent years!).
4. *Government purchases.*
Estimates of the value of these items in the national accounts are usually released quarterly by the Bureau of Economic Analysis, often seasonally adjusted and converted to an annual rate in order to make them more easily comparable.

A detailed explanation of the national accounts system is provided in *The U.S. Economy Demystified: What the Major Economic Statistics Mean and their Significance for Business,* by Albert T. Sommers (Lexington, Mass.: D.C. Heath and Company, 1985).

• • •

T.8 UPPERS AND DOWNERS: THE BUSINESS CYCLE

Economic growth fluctuates, and its ups and downs are usually described as part of a cycle of recession and recovery. Economists declare a *recession* when economic growth is negative (reflected in a declining GNP) for two consecutive quarters of a year. A *recession year* is a year in which the GNP is lower than it was in the previous year. The word *depression* is reserved for especially deep recessions that last a long time. There is no technical definition for a *recovery,* but the term usually refers to the period immediately after recession, when growth is restored.

Why is the economy plagued by a business cycle? At least a dozen explanations have been offered, including one that blames sunspots. But most economists agree that the business cycle is closely related to fluctuations in the level of business investment. That level is determined by expected costs and expected profits, both of which shift, in both predictable and unpredictable ways.

Because the business cycle has such an important impact on virtually all economic indicators, it's important to keep it in mind when interpreting economic statistics, and to make a distinction between short-run and long-run trends. Imagine, for instance, a beach at the ocean. If the water is calm and there are no waves, it's easy to tell whether the tide is moving in or out.

But a lot of waves can disguise the movement of the tide. To see which way it's going you might need to compare the distance from peak to peak (or from trough to trough) of several succeeding waves.

Economists sometimes call the long-term "tidal" changes *long waves* and describe the shorter waves as *cyclical* changes. Changes that are not cyclical are often termed *secular trends*.

T.9 A BRIEF GUIDE TO THE FEDERAL BUDGET

Every January, the president presents a proposed budget for the next fiscal year (FY) to Congress. For example, in January 1987, President Reagan submitted his budget for FY 1988, which runs from October 1, 1987, to September 30, 1988. This budget presents the administration's proposals for all the different programs of the federal government, including national defense, Social Security, Medicaid, and education. It explains and defends the spending required to meet the administration's objectives in all these areas. It also projects government revenues for the fiscal year and, consequently, the federal deficit. (A publication titled *The Budget in Brief* provides a summary of the budget.)

The president's budget remains only a proposal until it is passed by Congress and signed into law by the president. In recent years this process has often taken longer than twelve months (significantly past the beginning of the fiscal year it covers). The Gramm-Rudman-Hollings deficit-reduction bill, passed in 1985, is intended to speed up the decision-making process. Congress is now required to pass an initial budget resolution, setting targets for total spending and other major programs, revenues, and a reduced deficit, by April 15 of every year. By the end of August, appropriation bills for every program in the government's budget must be passed.

The Gramm-Rudman-Hollings bill also requires that, given projections for revenues, the overall deficit must be reduced by at least $38 billion every year until the budget is balanced in FY 1991. When Congress has completed its budget work, the president must sign all of the spending bills. If Congress and the president can't agree on spending totals (on overall military spending, for instance), the bill mandates automatic across-the-board cuts to meet the deficit-reduction targets. Some programs, such as Social Security and Medicare, are exempt from the automatic cuts, and the required cuts are to be split equally between defense and nondefense programs.

The federal budget process has a terminology (and logic) all its own. For instance, there is an important difference between budget authority and outlays. *Budget authority* describes a certain amount of money that is authorized for a particular program, which might last for several years, such as the B-1 bomber program. *Outlays,* on the other hand, refers to the actual amount of money spent out of the budget-authority "checking account" during a particular fiscal year. There's a big difference between the two. For example, in FY 1986, budget authority for national defense increased by about 3% while outlays increased by about 6%.

T.10 DEFINING THE POVERTY LINE

Feeling poor in the U.S. is not the same thing as officially *being* poor. The government includes a person or family among the poor if their income falls below an officially designated *poverty line* or *threshold,* which varies according to family size. In 1985 the poverty line for a family of four was $10,990; for a single person between the ages of 15 and 64, it was $5,590. Every year these thresholds are adjusted for inflation.

This official definition was pieced together in the 1950s from a patchwork of studies. Early Department of Agriculture surveys calculated the amount of money required for a subsistence diet. Another survey showed that the average family spent about one-third of its budget on food. So the poverty line was defined simply as the amount of money required for a subsistence diet multiplied by three.

Since that time, Department of Agriculture surveys have shown that the subsistence food budget originally designated is nutritionally inadequate for long-term use. They have also shown that the three-to-one ratio is no longer accurate and should be higher. Furthermore, the basic assumption that the poverty line can be defined in absolute, rather than in relative, terms is suspect. In 1960 the poverty line amounted to about 54% of *median family income,* but by 1984 had fallen to about 40%. In relative terms, poor families were much poorer in 1984 than before. But good methodological reasons for raising the poverty line have always been counteracted by political resistance to any change in definition that would increase the official poverty rate.

Revisions that would decrease the official poverty rate have received far more attention recently. Since the mid-1970s, government transfer programs have provided large amounts of noncash, or "in-kind" assistance, such as food stamps, Medicaid, and subsidized housing. It's difficult to estimate the market value of such benefits. For instance, if the money a poor person received through Medicaid were counted as though it were simply cash income, a person could escape official poverty by simply getting very sick. Still, the failure to include some estimate of noncash transfers in calculations of family income biases the official poverty line upward, and countervails at least some of the downward bias described above in years when noncash transfers are large.

Definitions of income and the poverty line affect assessments of trends as well as levels of poverty. If the full value of noncash transfers is added to measurements of family income (leaving the definition of the poverty line unchanged), the percentage of families with income under the poverty line is lowered. However, the increase in poverty between 1980 and 1985 is accentuated, because cuts in social spending diminished noncash transfers over that period.

SOURCES

▲ ▲

For a general guide to sources, see T.1. This list uses the following abbreviations:

BC: U.S. Bureau of the Census.
BLS: U.S. Bureau of Labor Statistics.
CPR: *Current Population Report,* BC (semimonthly).
EE: *Employment and Earnings,* U.S. Department of Labor (monthly).
EHE: *Employment, Hours, and Earnings, United States, 1909–1984,* vols. I and II, bulletin 1312-12, BLS.
ERP: *Economic Report of the President,* President's Council of Economic Advisors (annual).
FRB: *Federal Reserve Bulletin,* Board of Governors of the Federal Reserve System (monthly).
HLS: *Handbook of Labor Statistics,* U.S. Department of Labor (semiannual).
IRS: Internal Revenue Service.
MER: *Monthly Energy Review,* U.S. Energy Information Administration, Department of Energy (monthly).
MI: Various related titles of the *CPR* series on consumer income, P-60, such as *Money Income of Households, Families, and Persons in the United States.* For data from 1964 through 1978, the year was included after the word *Income,* and the rest of the time at the end of the title;

Money entered the title only in 1971; households were treated separately from 1967 to 1979, but were joined to families and persons in 1980.
MIPS: *Money Income and Poverty Status of Families and Persons in the United States,* a series of advance reports in the *CPR* series P-60 (annual).
NYT: *New York Times* (daily).
SA: *Statistical Abstract of the U.S.,* BC (annual).
SCB: *Survey of Current Business,* U.S. Department of Commerce.
WSJ: *Wall Street Journal* (daily, except weekends).

Chapter One: Owners.
  1.1 "Survey of Consumer Finances, 1983: A Second Report," *FRB,* Dec. 1984, p. 863, table 7. The distribution of families across income categories in this study was considerably different from that reported for a much larger sample in *MIPS 1985,* no. 154, p. 10, table 3. According to that source, in 1983, 15.6% of families had incomes over $50,000 and 25% under $15,000.
  1.2 Jeff Bloch, Christine Donahue, and Peter Newcomb, "The 400 Richest People in America," *Forbes,* Oct. 28, 1985, pp. 108–10.
  1.3 *MI 1983,* no. 146, Apr. 1985, p. 68, table 49. Text: IRS, *Statistics of Income, 1982* (Washington,

D.C.: General Printing Office, 1984), pp. 44–54.

1.4 "Survey of Consumer Finances, 1983," *FRB*, Sept. 1984, p. 689, table 13, and pp. 863–64.

1.5 Phillip Stern, testimony before the U.S. Senate on S.1878. Available from Citizens Against PACS, 2000 P Street N.W., rm. 408, Washington, D.C. 20036. Text: Charles McC. Mathias, "Federal Financing of Senate Campaigns," *NYT*, Nov. 22, 1985.

1.6 Data for fixed nonresidential private capital: *SA 1985*, p. 535, table 892. Reasoning used in calculating assets controlled from Lester Thurow, "The Leverage of Our Wealthiest 400," *NYT*, Oct. 11, 1984.

1.7 William G. Shepherd, *The Economics of Industrial Organization*, (Engelwood Cliffs, N.J.: Prentice Hall, 1985), pp. 117–18, and consultations with the author.

1.8 Data from "The 500 Largest U.S. Industrial Corporations," *Fortune*, for 1961: July 1962, pp. 172–78; for 1970: May 1971, pp. 172–78; for 1984: Apr. 29, 1985, pp. 268–72. Data for assets of nonfinancial corporations from *FRB*, for 1961: June 1962, p. 736; for 1970: Dec. 1971, p. A51; for 1984: July 1985, p. A36.

1.9 *ERP 1985*, p. 193, table 6.1. Data for 1984: W.T. Grimm and Co., *Mergerstat* (Chicago: 1985). Data for 1985: *NYT*, Dec. 29, 1985.

1.10 *NYT*, Dec. 29, 1985.

1.11 William A. Lovett, "The Revolution in U.S. Banking," *Challenge*, Nov.–Dec. 1984, p. 42.

1.12 John Stopford and John H. Dunning, *Multinationals: Company Performance and Global Trends* (London: Macmillan, 1983), p. 1. World Bank, *World Development Report, 1985*, p. 178, table 3.

1.13 Figures provided by the National Center for Employee Ownership, 927 South Walter Reed Drive #1, Arlington, Va. 22204.

1.14 Data for size of pension funds from Employee Benefit Research Institute, 2121 K Street N.W., Suite 860, Washington, D.C., 20037-2121. Data on percentage of stocks held from Richard A. Ippolito, *Pensions, Economics, and Public Policy* (Homewood, Illinois: Dow Jones-Irwin, 1986), p. 12.

Chapter Two: Workers

2.1 Data for 1950–82: *HLS*, bull. 2217, June 1985, pp. 8–9, table 2. Data for 1983–86: *EE*, Jan. 1987, p. 14, table A-2.

2.2 Data for goods and services, 1950–80: *EHE, pp. 7, 63. Data for 1987: EE*, Jan. 1987, p. 81, table B-1. Data for agriculture, 1950–80: *ERP 1986*, pp. 288–89, table B-31. Data for 1987: *EE*, Jan. 1987, p. 13, table A-1.

2.3 Data for 1950–80: *EHE*, pp. 58, 389, 390. Data for 1987: *EE*, Jan. 1987, p. 82, table, B-2. Data on number of employed, 1950–80: *ERP 1986*, pp. 288–89, table B-31. Data for 1987: *EE*, Jan. 1987, p. 43, table A-32.

2.4 Data for 1950–80: *EHE*, pp. 633–794. Data for 1987: *EE*, Jan. 1987, pp. 82–92, table B-2. Data for 1950: *ERP 1986*, pp. 388–89, table B-31. Data for 1987: *EE*, Jan. 1987, p. 43, table A-32. Text: data on money spent in restaurants from Bureau of Economic Analysis, Department of Commerce, *National Income and Product Accounts*, p. 89, table 2.4, and *SCB*, July 1985, p. 106, table 25.

2.5 Data on spendable earnings: Thomas E. Weisskopf, "Use of Hourly Earnings Proposed to Revive Spendable Earnings Series," *Monthly Labor Review*, Nov. 1984, p. 40, table 1. Data for earnings: *EHE*, vol. II; for 1985 earnings: *EE*, Jan. 1986, p. 79, table C-1; for 1986 earnings: *EE*, Jan. 1987, p. 117, table C-1.

2.6 Data for 1969–78: *HLS*, bull. 2060, Dec. 1980, p. 118, table 60. Data for 1979–83: *HLS*, bull. 2217, Dec. 1985, p. 94, table 41. Data for 1984–86: *EE*, Jan. 1986, p. 210, table 54, and Jan. 1987, p. 214, table 54.

2.7 *SA 1986*, p. 422, table 710.

2.8 Data for 1955–79: U.S. Chamber of Commerce, *Employee Benefits Historical Data* (Washington, D.C.: U.S. Chamber of Commerce Survey Research Center, 1981), p. 11, table 4. Data for 1985 obtained by telephone directly from Chamber of Commerce.

2.9 *EE*, Jan. 1987, p. 205, table 44. Text: *Pastoral Letter on Catholic Social Teaching and the U.S. Economy*, second draft, National Conference of Catholic Bishops, Washington, D.C., p. 41; Congressional Budget Office, *Economic and Budget Outlook: FY 1986–FY 1990*, February 1985, p. 75.

2.10 *EE*, Jan. 1987, p. 156, table 1; p. 197, table 35; p. 165, table A-7.

2.11 *ERP 1987*, p. 285, table B-35.

2.12 Johanna Moy, "Recent Trends in Unemployment and the Labor Force, 10 Countries," *Monthly Labor Review*, Aug. 1985, p. 14, table 2. Text: BLS, *International Comparisons of Unemployment* (1978), bull. 1979.

2.13 *HLS*, bull. 2217, June 1985, p. 80, table 32. Data for 1985: *ERP 1986*, p. 291, table B-33. Data for 1986: *EE*, Jan. 1987, p. 30, table A-15.

2.14 Paul O. Flaim and Ellen Seghal, "Displaced Workers of 1979–83: How Well Have They Fared?" *Monthly Labor Review*, June 1985, vol. 108, no. 6, pp. 3–16.

2.15 *EE*, Jan. 1987, p. 219, table 59; p. 220, table 60.

2.16 Data for 1950–78: *HLS*, bull. 2060, Dec. 1980, p. 412, table 165. Data for 1980: Larry T. Adams, "Changing Employment Patterns of Organized Workers," *Monthly Labor Review*, Feb. 1985, vol. 108, no. 2, p. 26. Data for 1983: *EE*, Jan.

1985, p. 209, table 53. Data for 1984: *EE,* Jan. 1986, p. 214, table 53. Data for 1985: *EE,* Jan. 1987 p. 219, table 59. Data for 1979, 1981, and 1982 are interpolated.

2.17 Data for inflation: *ERP 1987,* p. 311, table B-58. Data for wages, 1960–67: *HLS,* bull. 2217, June 1985, p. 331, table 102. Data for 1968–86, *Current Wage Developments,* Mar. 1986, p. 66 table 19. Text: Richard B. Freeman and James L. Medoff, *What Do Unions Do?* (New York: Basic Books, 1984); *15th Annual Report of the National Labor Relations Board,* Washington, D.C., table 2-A.

2.18 Juliet Schor and Samuel Bowles, "The Cost of Job Loss and the Incidence of Strikes," Harvard Institute of Economic Research, discussion paper no. 1105, November 1984.

Chapter Three: Women.

3.1 Data on white women and on black, Asian, and Native American women, 1955–82: *Employment and Training Report of the President, 1982,* pp. 155–57, table A-5. Data for 1983–86: *EE,* Jan. 1985, 1986, 1987, pp. 157, 159, tables 3 and 4. Data on married women with children under 6: BLS, *Labor Force Statistics Derived from the Current Population Survey: A Databook,* vol. 1, bull. 2096, Sept. 1982, p. 716, table C-11. Data for 1983–86: *SA 1986,* p. 399, table 675.

3.2 Victor R. Fuchs, "His and Hers: Gender Differences in Work and Income, 1959–1979," National Bureau of Economic Research, working paper no. 1501.

3.3 Data for 1960: *1970 Census, U.S. Summary,* sec. 2, pp. 718–24, table 21. Data for 1970 and 1980: *1980 Census,* pt. 1-A, pp. 166–75, table 276. Data for 1986: *EE,* Jan. 1987, p. 35, table A-22.

3.4 *EE,* Jan. 1987, p. 183, table 22. Text: Donald Treiman and Heidi I. Hartmann, eds., *Women, Work, and Wages: Equal Pay for Jobs of Equal Value* (Washington, D.C.: National Academy Press, 1981), p. 28.

3.5 Data for 1967, 1974: *SA 1985,* p. 419, table 700. Data for 1979: *HLS,* bull. 2217, June 1985, p. 94, table 41. Data for 1986: *EE,* Jan. 1987, p. 214, table 54.

3.6 Data for 1980–83: *SA 1985,* p. 419, table 700. Data of *EE,* Jan. 1987, p. 214, table 54.

3.7 U.S. Civil Rights Commission, *A Growing Crisis: Disadvantaged Women and Their Children,* Clearinghouse Publication 78, May 1983, p. 27, table 3.7.

3.8 International Labour Organization, *Yearbook of Labour Statistics, 1986* (Geneva), pp. 689–96, table 16.

3.9 *SA 1987,* p. 42, table 55.

3.10 *SA 1987,* p. 49, table 66. Text: Bureau of the Census, *Population Profile of the U.S.,* series P-23, no. 145, p. 18.

3.11 BC, *Child Support and Alimony, 1983,* series P-23, no. 141, p. 1.

3.12 Rebecca M. Blank and Allan S. Binder, "Macroeconomics, Income Distribution, and Poverty," Institute for Research on Poverty (University of Wisconsin, Madison) conference paper. BC, *Characteristics of Population Below Poverty Line,* series P-60, no. 147, June 1983, p. 178. Median maximum AFDC payment for a family of four in 1985: Children's Defense Fund, "A Children's Defense Budget FY 1986," Washington, D.C., pp. 272–73. Poverty line for family of four from Bureau of Census information office.

3.13 Series constructed by Randy Albelda and June Lapidus. See "Women and Children Last," in Center for Popular Economics, *Economic Report of the People* (Boston: South End Press, 1986), p. 64. Original data from *MI,* various years.

3.14 Data for 1985: *MIPS 1985,* no. 154, p. 21, table 15. Data for 1969: *1980 Census,* pp. 1–10W. Data for 1959: *MI,* no.115, July 1978, cover.

3.15 *SA 1986,* pp. 65–66, tables 102, 103. Linda Atkinson, Richard Lincoln, and Jacqueline Darroch Forrest, "Worldwide Trends in Funding for Contraceptive Research and Evaluation," *Family Planning Perspectives,* vol. 17, no. 5, Sept.–Oct. 1985, p. 196; "Fight on Teen-Age Pregnancy Asked," *NYT,* Nov. 5, 1985.

3.16 *WSJ,* May 14, 1987. See the forthcoming BC publication, *Who's Minding the Kids?* Text: Sheila B. Kamerman, Alfred J. Kahn, and Paul Kingston, *Maternity Policies and Working Women* (New York: Columbia University Press, 1983), p. 139. "Debate Over Pregnancy Leave," *NYT,* Feb. 3, 1986.

Chapter Four: People of Color

4.1 BC, *Estimates of the Population of the United States by Age, Sex, and Race: 1980–1985, CPR,* series P-25, no. 985, July 1985, p. 11, table 1; *Persons of Spanish Origin in the United States, March 1985, CPR,* series P-20, no. 403, Dec. 1985, p. 1.

4.2 *SA 1986,* p. 86, table 129; Muzaffer Christi, "Immigration Policy Examined," *Dollars and Sense,* June 1985, pp. 12–14.

4.3 *SA 1985,* p. 17, table 20.

4.4 Bureau of Indian Affairs, *American Indians* (Washington, D.C., 1984), pp. 27, 44; *Focus* (Institute for Research on Poverty, University of Wisconson, Madison), vol. 9, no. 1, Spring 1985, p. 25.

4.5 Data for 1972–84; *MI 1984, CPR, series P-60, no. 149, August 1985, p. 10, table 3.* Data for 1985: *SA 1985,* p.436, table 731.

4.6 Data for 1959 and 1974: *SA 1985,* p. 454, table

758. Data for 1985: *SA 1987*, p. 444, table 747.

4.7 Data for 1972–83: *HLS*, bull. 2217, June 1985, pp. 69–73, table 27. Data for 1984–86: Tom Nardone, BLS, Division of Employment and Unemployment Statistics. Text: *EE*, Jan. 1986, p. 160, table 6.

4.8 *EE*, Jan. 1987, p. 164, table 6.

4.9 *EE*, Apr. 1985, p. 73, table A-75.

4.10 Peter Bohmer, "The Impact of Public Sector Employment on Racial Inequality, 1950–1984," dissertation, University of Massachusetts, Sept. 1985, p. 202.

4.11 Data for 1956: *Income of Families and Persons in the U.S.: 1956, CPR*, series P-60, no. 27, p. 47, table 28. Data for 1970: *Income in 1970 of Families and Persons in the United States, CPR*, series P-60, no. 80, p. 129, table 59. Data for 1979: *SA 1985*, p. 434, no. 716. Data for 1986: *EE*, Jan. 1987, p. 214, table 54.

4.12 Peter Bohmer, "The Impact of Public Sector Employment on Racial Inequality, 1950–1984," dissertation, University of Massachusetts, Sept. 1985, pp. 55, 58.

4.13 *WSJ*, Oct. 24, 1985; *Annual Report of the Administrative Office of the U.S. Courts* (1981), p. 367; (1984) p. 254; D. Lee Bawden and John L. Palmer, "Social Policy: Challenging the Welfare State," in *The Reagan Record*, ed. John Palmer and Isabel Sawhill (Washington, D.C.: Urban Institute), p. 204.

4.14 *SA 1986*, p. 133, table 216.

4.15 *SA 1987*, p. 47, table 65.

4.16 Data for 1960 and 1970: *SA 1985*, p. 41, table 55. Data for 1985: *SA 1987*, p. 49, table 68.

4.17 *SA 1985*, p. 734, table 1313.

4.18 U.S. Department of Health and Human Services, *Health, U.S.* (1985), p. 41, table 12.

Chapter Five: Farmers

5.1 *ERP*, Feb. 1986, p. 362, table B-95. Text: Department of Agriculture, *Economic Indicators of the Farm Sector*, income and balance sheet statistics, 1983, p. 106.

5.2 *ERP*, Feb. 1986, p. 360, table B-93. Text: Department of Agriculture, *Economic Indicators of the Farm Sector*, national financial summary, 1984, pp. 40–41, tables 27, 28; BC, farm population series P-27, no. 58, p. 7, table F.

5.3 *SA 1986*, p. 652, table 1157. Text: Department of Agriculture, *Agricultural Handbook*, no. 637, 1984, p. 33; Todd S. Purdum, "R.J. Reynolds Set to Pay $4.9 Billion in Bid for Nabisco," *NYT*, June 3, 1985.

5.4 *ERP 1987*, p. 355, table B-96. Text: Department of Agriculture Economic Research Service, "History of Agricultural Price-Support and Adjustment Programs," *Agricultural Information Bulletin,* no. 485, p. 45.

5.5 *ERP 1987,* p. 357, table B-98. Text: "The Current Financial Condition of Farmers and Farm Lenders," *Agricultural Information Bulletin,* no. 490, p. 6.

5.6 Steven V. Roberts, "When Farm Interests Clash With the Budget," *NYT,* Nov. 10, 1985. Text: *NYT,* Mar. 6, 1985; *WSJ,* Feb. 19, 1986.

5.7 *ERP 1987,* pp. 352, 356, tables B-93, B-97.

5.8 *NYT,* May 25, 1986. Text: *NYT,* Apr. 20, 1986; May 25, 1986.

5.9 Data for 1974–84: SA 1986, p. 650, table 1154. Data for 1985: Department of Agriculture, *Report of Financial Condition and Operations of the Commodity Credit Corporation,* Jan. 1986, p. 4, exhibit B. Data for 1986: *NYT,* July 27, 1986. Text: *NYT,* July 27, 1986; *WSJ,* June 17, 1986.

5.10 World Bank, *World Development Report, 1985,* tables 1, 6, 24.

5.11 Department of Agriculture, *Hired Farm Workforce of 1985,* appendix table 8, and personal communication with Susan Pollack, Department of Agriculture.

5.12 *ERP 1987,* p. 354, table B-95.

Chapter Six: Government Spending

6.1 *ERP 1987,* pp. 244, 335, tables B-1, B-76.

6.2 U.S. Advisory Commission on Intergovernmental Relations, *Significant Features of Fiscal Federalism,* 1985–86 edition, p. 132, table 79.

6.3 Data for Germany and Japan: Peter Saunders, Frederick Klau, "The Role of the Public Sector," *Economic Studies* (Organization for Economic Cooperation and Development), no. 4, Spring 1985, p. 52. Data for U.S. based on: *ERP 1985,* pp. 262, 343, tables B-8, B-76; *SA 1985,* p. 269, table 445; *Historical Guide to the U.S. Budget, FY 1986,* 3.3(1)-3.3(30), table 3.3.

6.4 Office of Management and Budget, *Historical Tables, Budget of the United States Government, FY 1986,* pp. 3.1(5)-3.1(6), table 3.1

6.5 Ibid., pp. 3.3(4), table 3.3.

6.6 Ibid., pp. 3.3(14), table 3.3.

6.7 Ibid., pp. 3.3(9)–3.3(19), table 3.3.

6.8 Ibid., pp. 3.3(19), table 3.3.

6.9 *SA 1986,* p. 266, table 446.

6.10 Data on corporate income tax: Office of Management and Budget, *Historical Tables, FY 1988,* p. 2.1(2), table 2.1; Data on corporate profits: *ERP 1987,* table B-84.

6.11 Data for personal income: *ERP 1987,* p. 272, table B-24, and same table, previous years. Data for individual income and Social Security tax: *ERP 1987,* p. 333, table B-74, and same table, previous years.

6.12 *WSJ*, June 25, 1986; *NYT*, Aug. 18, 1986.

6.13 *ERP 1987*, p. 335, table B-76.

6.14 *ERP 1987*, pp. 244, 332–33, tables B-1, B-74.

Chapter Seven: Welfare, Education, and Health

7.1 Data for 1950–82: *MI 1983*, no. 146, p. 41, table 15. Data for 1983, 1984: *MIPS 1984*, no. 149, p. 9, table 2. Data for 1985: *MIPS 1985*, no. 154, p. 10, table 3.

7.2 *MI 1983*, no. 146, p. 50, table 17; *MIPS 1984*, no. 149, p. 11, table 4; *MIPS 1985*, no. 154, p. 11, table 4.

7.3 Data for 1967–1982: *Characteristics of the Population Below the Poverty Line, 1982, CPR*, series P-60, no. 144, Mar. 1984, p. 7, table 1. Data for 1983–84: *MIPS 1984*, no. 149, pp. 21–23, table 15. Data for 1985: *MIPS 1985*, no. 154, p. 22, table 16.

7.4 *MIPS 1985*, no. 154, p. 3, table B.

7.5 *NYT*, Mar. 6, 1986. Text: Sheldon Danziger and Peter Gottschalk, "How Have Families with Children Been Faring?" Institute for Research on Poverty, University of Wisconsin, Madison. Testimony prepared for the Joint Economic Committee of the United States Congress, Nov. 1985.

7.6 Data for 1959: *Social Security Bulletin, Annual Statistical Supplement*, 1983, p. 66. Data for 1974: BC, *Population Profile of the United States, 1982*, series P-23, no. 130, Dec. 1983, pp. 74–75. Data for 1985: *MIPS 1985*, no. 154, p. 22, table 16.

7.7 *Characteristics of the Population Below the Poverty Level, 1984, CPR*, series P-60, no. 152, p. 69, table 19. Text: "Poking Holes in Some Myths About the Poor," *Business Week*, May 5, 1985, p. 16.

7.8 Greg J. Duncan, *Years of Poverty, Years of Plenty* (Ann Arbor: University of Michigan Institute for Social Research, 1984), p. 77. Text: "Poking Holes"; *Population Profile of the United States, 1983/84*, CPR, series P-23, no. 145, p. 32.

7.9 Data for pre-transfer: Sheldon Danziger and Peter Gottschalk, "The Poverty of Losing Ground," *Challenge,* May–June 1985, p. 34, table 1. Data for post-transfer: *MIPS 1984*, no. 149, p. 21, table 15.

7.10 *MIPS 1985*, no. 154, p. 32, table 21.

7.11 *SA 1987*, p. 716, table 1293. Text: Jim Wright, "No, You Can't Have It All," *NYT*, Feb. 3, 1986; Gale Cincotta, letter from National People's Action, Chicago, *NYT*, May 3, 1986.

7.12 *NYT*, Feb. 19, 1986; *Newsweek*, Jan. 6, 1986; *NYT*, Jan. 22, 1986.

7.13 Data for 1970–81: Donald A. Gillespie and Nancy Carlson, *Trends in Student Aid, 1963–83*, Washington Office of the College Board, table 1, p. 5. Data for 1985–87: "A Report from the

Washington Office of the College Board," Jan. 1987, p. 6, table 1.

7.14 Data for 1975–86: SA 1987, p. 126, table 208. Data for teachers in 1986 from the National Educational Association.

7.15 *SA 1987*, p. 98, table 150.

7.16 Data by race and ethnicity: *Disability, Functional Limitation, and Health Insurance Coverage, 1984/85, CPR*, series P-70, no. 8, p. 10, table I. Data by household type: *Economic Characteristics of Households in the United States, Fourth Quarter 1984, CPR*, series P-70, no. 6, Jan. 1986, p. 3.

7.17 *A Children's Defense Budget: An Analysis of the President's Fiscal 1987 Budget and Children,* (Washington, D.C.: Children's Defense Fund, 1986), p. 343; *SA 1986*, pp. 374, 458, tables 634, 767.

7.18 *WSJ*, Jan. 28, 1986; *NYT*, Jan. 22, 1986.

Chapter Eight: Environment and Energy

8.1 *MER*, Jan. 1987, p. 7, table 1.4

8.2 Annual Report, Exxon, Jan. 1984; *MER*, Jan. 1987, p. 13, table 1.8.

8.3 *MER*, Jan. 1987, p. 91, table 9.1. Text: *WSJ*, May 23, 1986.

8.4 *MER*, Feb. 1984, p. 13, table 1.8.

8.5 *NYT*, May 4, 1986. Text: *NYT*, May 2, 25, 1986.

8.6 James Everett Katz, *Congress and National Energy Policy* (New Brunswick: Transaction Books, 1984), p. 163. Text: Christopher Flavin and Cynthia Pollock, "Harnessing Renewable Energy," *State of the World*, Lester Brown, ed., (New York: W.W. Norton, 1985) pp. 172, 198.

8.7 *SA 1986*, p. 842, table 1472; p. 851, table 1490.

8.8 Henry Kendall and Steven Nadis, eds., *Energy Strategies: Toward a Solar Future, A Report of the Union of Concerned Scientists* (Cambridge: Ballinger 1980), p. 287, fig. 6.1

8.9 *SA 1985*, p. 202, fig. 7.2. Text: Jonathan Lash, Katherine Gillman, and David Sheridan, *A Season of Spoils* (New York: Pantheon, 1984), p. 102; *WSJ*, May 16, 1985.

8.10 *Environmental Quality 1984: The Fifteenth Annual Report of the Council on Environmental Quality*, p. 612, table A-18.

8.11 *SA 1986*, p. 190, table 332. Text: Sandra Postel, "Protecting Forests from Air Pollution and Acid Rain," *State of the World 1985*, p. 10.

8.12 *NYT*, July 2, 1985. Text: *NYT*, Sept. 17, 1985.

8.13 *SA 1987*, p. 189, table 329.

8.14 *Environmental Quality 1984*, pp. 16 and 21.

8.15 A. Myrick Freeman III, *Air and Water Pollution Control* (New York: John Wiley and Sons, 1982), pp. 129–30, 169; Joseph Seneca and Michael Taussig, *Environmental Economics* (Englewood Cliffs: Prentice-Hall, 1984), p. 121.

8.16 *Los Angeles Times*, Oct. 11, 1983; *WSJ*, Jan. 25,

1984 and Apr. 10, 1979; *Christian Science Monitor*, Dec. 31, 1981; *NYT*, May 2, 1986.

8.17 *SA 1987* p. 193, table 340.

8.18 Office of Management and Budget, *Historical Tables, Budget, 1987*, p. 3.2(3)–(6), table 3.2. Text: Lash, Gillman, and Sheridan, *A Season of Spoils*, pp. 59, 69, 235.

Chapter Nine: Macroeconomics

9.1 *ERP 1987*, p. 251, table B-5.

9.2 *ERP 1987*, p. 285, table B-35.

9.3 *ERP 1987*, p. 312, table B-59.

9.4 *ERP 1987*, pp. 285, 312, tables B-35, B-59.

9.5 *ERP 1987*, pp. 285, 295, tables B-35, B-44..

9.6 For a more detailed explanation of this aspect of the business cycle see Samuel Bowles and Richard Edwards, *Understanding Capitalism: Competition, Command, and Change in the U.S. Economy* (New York: Harper and Row, 1985).

9.7 *ERP 1987*, pp. 251, 324, tables B-5, B-68.

9.10 Robert Eisner, "Will the Real Federal Deficit Please Stand Up?" *Challenge*, May/June 1986, pp. 16–17.

9.11 *ERP 1986*, pp. 253, 270, 276, 311, tables B-1, B-15, B-21, B-51.

9.12 *ERP 1987*, p. 294, table B-43.

9.13 *ERP 1987*, p. 360, table B-91.

9.14 *ERP 1987*, p. 343, table B-84; *SCB*, Jan. 1986, pp. 54–55, table 2, and Aug. 1986, p. 36, table 2.

9.15 *ERP 1987*, p. 274, table B-25.

9.16 Federal Reserve Bank, Flow-of-Funds Department, unpublished data. Slightly less up-to-date estimates are published annually in *ERP*, table B-69. GNP estimates from *ERP 1987*, p. 244, table B-1.

Chapter Ten: The Global Economy

10.1 *ERP 1987*, p. 368, table B-108.

10.2 Data for 1951-80: *OECD National Accounts*, vol. 1, 1951–80, ed. 1982, pp. 30, 32, 48, 68, 74. Data for 1981–84: United Nations, *National Accounts Statistics: Main Aggregates and Detailed Tables*, 1984, pp. 563, 835, 1602, 1649.

10.3 Department of Labor, *International Comparisons of Manufacturing Productivity and Labor Cost Trends, Preliminary Measures for 1984*, revised tables, June 10, 1985, news release, p. 2, table A.

10.4 *BLS*, Office of Productivity and Technology. Less up-to-date estimates are found in *HLS*, bull. 2217, June 1985, p. 435, table 132.

10.5 Data for total goods produced: *ERP 1987*, pp. 252, 358, tables B-6, B-99. Export and import data: Council of Economic Advisers, *Economic Indicators*, Apr. 1987, p. 36.

10.6 "Protectionism Isn't Such a Dirty Word Anymore," *Business Week*, Oct. 7, 1985, pp. 95–96.

10.7 Data for 1950–85: *ERP 1987*, p. 358. Data for

1986: *Economic Indicators,* Apr. 1987, p. 36. *Goods and services* is defined as the sum of net merchandise exports and net travel and transportation receipts. *Investment income* is the sum of net investment income and other services, net.

10.8 *FRB,* Mar. 1987, p. A-68, and similar tables in previous issues.

10.9 Data for 1950–76: Bureau of Economic Analysis, *National Income and Product Accounts,* Sept. 1981, table 6.23b. Data for 1977–81: *SCB,* July 1984, p. 79, table 6.23b. Data for 1982–85: *SCB,* July 1986, p. 77, table 6.21b.

10.10 Same as 10.7.

10.11 *ERP 1985,* p. 356, table B-109.

10.12 World Bank, *World Development Report, 1985,* p. 174, table 1.

10.13 *World Development Report, 1985,* pp. 218–19, table 23; pp. 222–23, table 25. Data for 1983 per-capita GNP for Cuba estimated by Andrew Zimbalist, Department of Economics, Smith College.

10.14 "Foreign Assistance and Related Programs. Appropriations for 1986," hearings before a subcommittee of the Committee on Appropriations, House of Representatives, Ninety-Ninth Congress, p. 4, table II, foreign assistance summary table.

10.15 Data for 1977: International Monetary Fund, *World Economic Outlook,* April 1985, p. 267, table 45. Data for 1980, 1986: *Outlook,* April 1986, p. 243, table A47.

10.16 World Bank, *World Development Report, 1986* (New York: Oxford University Press, 1987), pp. 214–15, table 18.

GLOSSARY

▲ ▲

Acid rain. Highly acidic rain, resulting from the emission of sulfur, nitrogen oxides, and other pollutants.

Adjusted full-employment deficit. A measure of what the federal budget deficit would be under hypothetical conditions of full employment.

Affirmative action. A program to remedy the effects of past racial or sexual discrimination in employment. Unlike anti-discrimination or equal-opportunity laws, which forbid unequal treatment, affirmative action requires positive corrective measures. Employment goals and timetables are established to increase the participation of underrepresented groups of people.

Aid to Families with Dependent Children (AFDC). Financial aid for families of children living with a sole parent or relative who lacks adequate income. In some states, families with both parents present are eligible if the primary wage earner is unemployed. The program is administered by the states with the assistance of federal funds and under federal regulations.

Antitrust law. Legislation designed to restrict the market power exercised by firms. When individual firms, groups of amalgamated companies (trusts), or groups of cooperating firms (cartels) have considerable market power, they can restrict competition and raise prices.

Asset. Anything of value that is owned. See also **financial asset.**

Baby boom. The period of high birth rates in the U.S. from the end of World War II through 1964.

Balance of payments. The difference between the total payments into and out of a country during a given period. It includes all merchandise trade, tourist expenditures, capital movements, and interest charges.

Bond. An IOU or promissory note from a corporation or government. A bond certifies a debt on which the issuer (borrower) agrees to pay a specified amount of interest over a specified period of time, and to repay the principal on the date of expiration or maturity. Bonds are issued to raise capital. There are many types: the federal government sells treasury bonds, local governments sell municipal bonds, and corporations sell corporate bonds in order to raise capital.

Bracket creep. When tax rates depend on income level, inflation can lead to increases in income that can shift an individual into a higher tax bracket. Taxpayers can end up paying much higher taxes even though their real income has not increased.

Bureau of Labor Statistics. One of the seven major sections of the Department of Labor. The principal fact-finding agency on labor economics issues.

Business cycle. The pattern of medium-term economic fluctuations, marked by alternating periods of expansion and recession. See 6.1.

Capital gain. The difference between the purchase price of an asset and its higher resale price at some later date. A **capital loss** occurs when the resale price is less than the purchase price.

Capital goods. Durable goods needed in the production of other goods and services, such as factories, machinery, and equipment.

Capitalist. One who owns capital goods and exercises control over the labor of others. He or she receives income in the form of profits.

Capital stock. The sum of capital goods in an economy.

Child-support payments. Payments made by one parent to another for the purpose of maintaining their child's welfare. Sometimes a divorce settlement will include both alimony (to support an ex-spouse) and child-support payments.

Commercial banks. Privately owned banks that receive deposits and make loans. They also operate trust departments, act as agents in buying and selling securities, and underwrite and sell new security issues for state and local governments. All U.S. national banks and some state banks are commercial banks.

Commodity Credit Corporation. Established in 1933 and now part of the U.S. Department of Agriculture, the Commodity Credit Corporation, along with the Agricultural Stabilization and Conservation Service, provides cash assistance to farmers by making loans, buying crops, and making direct payments.

Comparable worth. A method of setting wages and salaries across occupations that is based on statistical analysis of certain common characteristics of jobs, such as responsibility and working conditions. Also called **pay equity.**

Concentration. The extent to which an industry is dominated by a small number of firms. The concentration ratio measures the percentage of total assets, production, employment, sales, or profits in the hands of top firms.

Conglomerate. A corporation engaged in many unrelated industries. A conglomerate often acquires its large, diversified holdings through mergers or takeovers.

Consumer price index (CPI). The cost of a "market basket" of about four hundred goods and services purchased by a typical household relative to its cost in a base year. The index is calculated and reported monthly by the Bureau of Labor Statistics.

Corporation. An association of business owners, called stockholders, who are regarded as a single entity (or person) in the eyes of the law. The chief advantages of the corporation are limited liability (each stockholder is liable for the debts of the business only to the extent of his or her investment), easy transfer of ownership (anyone can buy or sell stock at any time), and continuity or performance (the corporation continues to exist even if all the owners die). Created by statute law, which varies from state to state, a corporation has no legal status outside of the state in which it is chartered.

Cost-of-living allowance (COLA). A wage increase (usually based on a consumer price index) given to all employees during an inflationary period to keep their pay in line with the cost of living.

Cost of production. The total cost of materials, labor, and overhead charges such as rent and electricity incurred in production.

Debt service. The interest and charges due on a debt, including principal payments.

Demand. The quantity of a commodity that one consumer or all consumers would be willing and able to buy.

Department of Energy (DOE). Established in 1977, the DOE has primary responsibility for finding and developing new energy sources, encouraging conservation, coping with the impact of energy problems, and administering other policies and programs in the energy field. It also manages the nuclear-weapons program and major power-generating programs.

Depreciation. The cost of restoring the wear and tear, aging, or technological obsolescence of the capital goods used in producing (a year's) output.

Depression. A prolonged period of very reduced business activity. Production and new capital investment are greatly scaled back, income is sharply lowered, unemployment is massive, and many businesses fail.

Deregulation. The reduction of government control over the operations of various industries. In the late 1970s this policy was applied to the transportation industries (airlines, air freight, trucking, railroads) and financial institutions (commercial banks, thrift institutions, brokerage houses).

Direct foreign investment. Buying or establishing a controlling interest in a foreign business or subsidiary, usually involving managerial control and technological input.

Discount rate. The interest rate charged by the Federal Reserve on loans to member banks. Discount rates are set every two weeks by the regional Fed banks, subject to approval by the board of governors.

Discouraged workers. Workers so disheartened by a fruitless search for employment that they stop looking and withdraw from the labor force. The official unemployment rate is understated because these people are not counted.

Dividends. A payment to stockholders in a company, in either cash or stock, in proportion to their share of ownership.

Dow-Jones Industrial Average. An average of stock prices that serves as a barometer of the market as a whole. This average is based on thirty industrial stocks.

Durable good. A good that can be used repeatedly—for instance, a car.

Economic expansion. The phase of a business cycle when total output and employment rise.

Employee Stock Ownership Plan (ESOP). Also called **stock-purchase plan,** an ESOP permits employees to purchase stock in the company that employs them by means of payroll deductions, often at a discount from the current market price. See 1.13.

Environmental Protection Agency (EPA). An independent federal agency created in 1970 to deal with pollution in the areas of air, water, solid waste, noise, radiation, and toxic substances.

Equal Employment Opportunities Commission. An independent federal agency established by the Civil Rights Act of 1964 to help end racial and sexual discrimination in employment practices and promote voluntary affirmative action. The commission stresses confidential persuasion and conciliation. Though authorized in 1972 to take legal actions if conciliation fails, the commission can't issue cease-and-desist orders.

Export. Any good or service sold to a foreign country.

Farm inputs. Seed, fertilizer, tractors, and other goods, used in the production of farm outputs, such as food.

Farmers Home Administration (FHA). A branch of the Department of Agriculture that makes loans to farmers to buy farms, and to cover operating expenses, emergencies resulting from natural disasters, soil and water conservation projects, and rural housing.

Federal budget deficit. A deficit occurs when the government spends more than it takes in through taxes.

Federal Reserve. The central bank of the United States, responsible for maintaining and enhancing the viability and stability of the monetary system. The Federal Reserve Board presides over twelve Federal Reserve banks in different areas of the country. See 9.8.

Federal Reserve member bank. All national banks and about 40% of all state commercial banks that are regulated by the Federal Reserve system and receive services from it, such as check clearing, holding member-bank reserve accounts, and extending credit.

Federal retirement and disability system. See **Social Security.**

Financial asset. A security such as a stock, a bond, or a government Treasury bill.

Firm. A business entity. Proprietorships (owned by one person), partnerships (owned by two or more people), and corporations (owned by stockholders) are all firms.

Fiscal policy. Using government spending and taxation to affect some aspect of the economy, especially levels of unemployment and inflation.

Food stamps. A welfare program to improve nutrition in low-income households. The program is administered by the Department of Agriculture through state and local welfare agencies, which establish eligibility, issue stamps, and maintain controls.

Full-employment GNP. A measure of the value of goods and services that could be produced if the country's factors of production (labor and capital) were fully employed.

Golden parachutes. Income and benefits guaranteed to executives in case they are dismissed when control of the firm is transferred, as in a takeover.

Government transfers (transfer payments). Payments made by the state to needy individuals that, in effect, transfer income from wealthier sectors of the population to the poorer. No productive service is required in return.

Gross domestic product. A measure of the total value of goods and services produced in a country over a specified time period, normally a year. Neither the value of imports nor the income from investments abroad is included.

Gross national product (GNP). The value of the goods and services bought and sold in an economy during a given time period, normally a year. It is used as a measure of a nation's economic activity.

Householder. The designated "reference person" to whom the relationship of all other household members is recorded. The householder is the person (or one of the persons) in whose name the housing unit is owned or rented.

Import. Any good or service bought from a foreign country.

Industrial goods. See **capital goods.**

Infant mortality rate. The number of infants per thousand births who die within the first year of life.

Inflation. A general increase in prices, often measured by an increase in the consumer price index.

Investment (capital). Buying capital goods that will be used directly in the production of goods and services, such as a plant or equipment.

Investment (financial). Buying any financial asset, such as a stock or bond.

Investment tax credit. A percentage of the cost of a new plant or equipment that businesses are allowed to deduct from their taxes to encourage them to invest.

Junk bonds. High-risk, unsecured bonds issued by a firm. In the event of bankruptcy, holders of junk bonds are the last creditors to receive money back, if they receive any at all. Junk bonds are sometimes issued by a corporation needing a large amount of cash in order to buy out another company.

Labor force. All civilians sixteen years and older who have jobs or are actively looking for jobs.

Labor-force participation rate. The proportion of the population of working age that is part of the labor force.

Leading indicator. An indicator that anticipates the ups and downs of the business cycle. Among the twelve considered most important are the average number of hours production workers worked per week, average weekly new claims for state unemployment insurance, new orders for consumer and capital goods and the money supply.

Macroeconomics. The study of the behavior of the economy as a whole, focusing on variables such as employment, inflation, growth, and stability. See Chapter Nine.

Marginal tax rate. The tax rate on the income beyond a given point—the marginal income. If the tax rate on the first $1000 is 10% ($100) and the marginal tax rate on the second (marginal) $1000 is 20% ($200), then the total tax paid is $300, for an average tax rate of 15%.

Mean. See T.3.

Median. See T.3.

Medicaid. Poor persons who need medical services but do not qualify for Medicare are assisted under this federally supported state system.

Medicare. A health insurance program established as an amendment to the Social Security Act to provide medical care for the elderly. Two health-care programs are involved. The first, which is compulsory and financed by increases in the Social Security payroll tax, covers most hospital and nursing-home costs for persons aged 65 or older. The second is a voluntary supplemental health program for persons over 65, which covers a variety of health services both in and out of medical institutions and pays a substantial part of physician costs. The supplemental plan is financed by a small charge to the person enrolled and by an equal amount paid by the federal government out of general revenue.

Merger. The fusion of two or more separate companies into one. In current usage, merger is a special case where the merging companies wish to join together and do so on roughly equal terms.

Minimum wage. The lowest wage, established by law or contract, which can be paid by an employer. In addition to the federal minimum wage, some states have minimum wages.

Monetary policy. The use of monetary controls—restricting or expanding the money supply or manipulating the interest rate—to achieve some objective, such as controlling inflation, improving the balance of payments, achieving a certain level of employment, or increasing the GNP.

Monopoly. Strictly speaking, a monopoly exists when a firm or individual produces and sells the entire output of some commodity. The lack of competition gives that firm market power.

Multinational corporation (MNC). A company that has operation centers in many countries. An international company, on the other hand, imports or exports goods but has its operation centered in one country.

National Labor Relations Board (NLRB). A federal agency that administers the laws relating to labor relations in the private and nonprofit sectors. The NLRB has the power to safeguard the rights of employees to organize, to determine through elections whether they want union representation, and to prevent or remedy unfair labor practices.

Net national product. The value of the total output of goods and services within a given time period, usually a year, less the costs of depreciation and capital goods used up.

Net worth. The total assets of a person or business less the total amount due to creditors (liabilities).

Nondurable goods. Goods that wear out after a few uses, seldom lasting more than a couple of years—for instance, a pair of shoes.

Nonfinancial corporate asset. Any asset owned by a corporation that is not financial. These include plants, equipment, inventories, and accounts receivable.

Nuclear Regulatory Commission (NRC). An independent regulatory body created in 1974 to license and regulate civilian and military use of nuclear power. It has assumed primary responsibility for maintaining secrecy, security, scientific and engineering safeguards, and environmental control.

Oligopoly. A market situation in which there are only a few producers of a good or service. The relative lack of competition gives the firms some market power and makes it easier for them to collude.

Organization of Petroleum Exporting Countries (OPEC). An international organization that coordinates petroleum production and pricing policies in member countries. The organization was formally established in 1960. It negotiates petroleum prices, sets production ceilings, and provides financial assistance for developing countries. Member nations include Iran, Iraq, Kuwait, Libya, Saudi Arabia, Venezuela, Algeria, Ecuador, Gabon, Indonesia, Nigeria, Qatar, and the United Arab Emirates.

Pay equity. See **comparable worth.**

Pension fund. Money laid aside and normally invested to provide a regular income upon retirement, or in case of disability.

Pink collar. Occupations such as nursing or secretarial jobs in which a high percentage of workers have traditionally been and continue to be women.

Poison pills. When a firm does not want to be acquired or taken over it will sometimes issue a significant amount of high risk debt in order to make itself look less attractive to a potential buyer—a poison pill of debt.

Political action committee (PAC). Usually a group of paid professionals that lobbies Congress to pass laws or to keep laws on the books that are beneficial to a particular interest. PACs raise substantial amounts of money and donate this money to the candidates of their choice.

Poverty line. See T.10.

Poverty rate. The percentage of the population with incomes under the poverty line. See T.10.

Price supports. A system of agricultural support by which prices are fixed above market-determined levels. The federal government buys unsold surpluses, thus supporting the price and raising farmers' income.

Production workers. Workers engaged in actual production, as opposed to supervision.

Productive capacity. The potential output of a business with existing plant, workers, and equipment.

Productivity. The efficiency with which productive resources are used. The term is most commonly applied to labor.

Profit rate. The ratio of a company's profits to the value of its capital stock.

Progressive tax. A tax in which the rate rises with income. Most income-tax systems in Western countries are progressive.

Protectionism. The policy of imposing restrictions such as tariffs (taxes) or quotas (quantity limits) on imported goods in order to protect domestic industries.

Public sector. That part of the economy that is publicly rather than privately owned. It includes all government departments and agencies and all public corporations such as electricity and water boards.

Real earnings. Earnings after the effects of inflation have been taken into account. See T.4.

Real interest rate. The interest rate minus the anticipated rate of inflation—what a borrower is actually paying for the use of money.

Recession. That part of the business cycle in which total output falls. During a recession, investment usually declines and the unemployment rate rises.

Renewable sources of energy. Energy sources that are not depleted when they are used, such as solar power.

Reserve army of labor. The reserve of workers that want a job but are unable to find one.

Revenue-neutral. A revenue-neutral tax bill is one that neither generates additional tax revenue taken in by the government nor reduces it.

Safety-net programs. Programs that guarantee some minimum level of security or protection from poverty.

Savings. All income not spent on goods and services used for current consumption. Both firms and households save.

Social Security. Officially known as the **Old-Age, Survivors, and Disability Insurance (OASDI),** its major purposes are to provide a retirement income for elderly persons, income for workers who are totally disabled, income for spouses and children of deceased wage earners, and medical care for the aged (Medicare). All eligible workers are required to contribute a certain percent of their income, which is matched by their employer. These payments are credited to the account of each worker, and upon death, retirement, or disablement, funds are allocated in accordance with the formulas provided by law.

Social spending. A category of spending by government agencies to increase the welfare of individuals and the community as a whole. As used in this book, the term does not include expenditures on Social Security and Medicare.

Spendable earnings. Earnings after all taxes have been deducted.

Stagflation. A combination of stagnation (slow growth and high unemployment) and inflation (rising prices).

Standard of living. The level of material well-being of an individual or household.

Stocks. Certificates or claims of ownership in a corporation. Types of stocks vary. Some entitle owners to dividends and to voting rights.

Supply-side economics. An economic theory that emphasizes the potential impact of tax cuts and deregulation on increasing the supply of goods and services produced. This theory de-emphasizes the importance of the demand for goods and services.

Tax loophole. A legal provision that can be used to reduce one's tax liability. Such provisions may be unintentional discrepancies in the law, or they may be intended to benefit an industry or group.

Trade deficit. The amount by which a nation's imports exceed its exports or merchandise over a given period.

Unemployment insurance. An insurance program established by the Social Security Act of 1935 that for a limited period of time pays workers who are temporarily laid off or permanently discharged for reasons beyond their control. Under the plan, Congress imposes a tax on the payroll of firms that employ four or more workers. All proceeds are held by the Treasury Department in separate state accounts to be paid out as needed by each state. Each state determines the amount to be paid to each unemployed person, for how long, and under what conditions.

Value of the dollar. The worth of the U.S. dollar in terms of a foreign country's currency.

Worker participation. A form of workplace democracy that enables workers to exercise power over a firm's decisions.